W9-APT-107

My Days in Court

My Days in Court

Unique Views of the Famous and Infamous by a Court Artist

IDA LIBBY DENGROVE
and FRANK W. MARTIN

William Morrow and Company, Inc.
New York

358736

Copyright © 1990 by Ida Libby Dengrove and Frank W. Martin

All rights reserved. No part of this book may be reproduced or utilized in any form or by any means, electronic or mechanical, including photocopying, recording or by any information storage and retrieval system, without permission in writing from the Publisher. Inquiries should be addressed to Permissions Department, William Morrow and Company, Inc., 105 Madison Avenue, New York, N.Y. 10016.

Recognizing the importance of preserving what has been written, it is the policy of William Morrow and Company, Inc., and its imprints and affiliates to have the books it publishes printed on acid-free paper, and we exert our best efforts to that end.

Library of Congress Cataloging-in-Publication Data

Dengrove, Ida Libby.
My days in court : unique views of the famous and infamous by a court artist / Ida Libby Dengrove and Frank W. Martin.
p. cm.
ISBN 0-688-08706-X
1. Dengrove, Ida Libby. 2. Illustrators—United States—Biography. 3. Courtroom art—United States. I. Martin, Frank W. II. Title.
NC953.8.D46A2 1990
741′.092—dc20
[B] 89-49316
CIP

Printed in the United States of America

First Edition

1 2 3 4 5 6 7 8 9 10

BOOK DESIGN BY JAYE ZIMET

To my husband, Ed,
for his love and support
and
To Radmila and Mary Ann,
for their golden hearts

Acknowledgments

The authors wish to express their gratitude to a talented group of people whose contributions enlivened the pages of this book. Special thanks to Robert Eringer for his perspective and support, to the librarians at Monmouth (New Jersey) College for their help in obtaining vital research material, to Pat Golbitz for her skilled editing, to Jill Hamilton for her encouragement and patience, and to Bill Drennan for his thoroughness.

Preface

COURTROOM ILLUSTRATOR IDA LIBBY DENGROVE SAT through the most celebrated court proceedings in the country. For fifteen years, her sketches of defendants, witnesses, lawyers, and judges were often society's only visual link with what went on in the courtroom.

Ida brought a special dimension to courtroom illustration. "Her sketches," said Judge Russell Leggett about Dengrove's work during the murder trial of Jean Harris, "were the best I've ever seen. Although other artists were dedicated, conscientious, and accurate, Ida possessed the additional quality of capturing the inner feelings of the person she was sketching."

That was her trademark. She never claimed objectivity in her work. On the contrary, Ida Libby Dengrove saw, felt, and portrayed the vast range of human emotions that took place in the courtroom. Hers was a prejudiced viewpoint. She interpreted rather than recorded events as they unfolded. She sought and got the human element. She studied the defendant. She looked at everything: clothing, body language, eyes, emotional state.

That's what made Dengrove's sketches so powerful. She instantly assimilated a psychological profile of the defendant and transferred that image to her sketchbook. Ida was not bound by journalistic restraints. A professionally trained artist, she had no legal or media bias. She absorbed the courtroom mood and scene in a way that no reporter, no photographer, and no cameraman ever could, because her mission—to capture visually the passion of the courtroom—was so different.

Dengrove provided television viewers and newspaper readers with provocative images of the rich, the famous, the notorious, and even the disgusting people who paraded through the nation's court system.

As the chief illustrator for WNBC in New York City and NBC News from 1972 to 1987, she sketched such disparate personalities as actress Brooke Shields and Ayatollah Khomeini and events ranging from the Georgetown, Guyana, trial of Larry Layton, accused of killing a congressman and two newsmen before the Jonestown massacre, to the deportation hearings of John Lennon and Yoko Ono.

Ida was twice awarded television's highest honor, receiving an Emmy Award for Outstanding Individual Craft for her chilling courtroom sketches of David ("Son of Sam") Berkowitz and Craig ("Murder at the Met") Crimmins. She also was nominated twice more for her stunning portraiture during the tax evasion trial of the Reverend Sun Myung Moon and during the verdict announcement at the Brinks robbery trial.

In addition to her work in the courtroom, Dengrove did "reconstructions" based on eyewitness observations of scenes that could not be recorded by television cameras—the aborted hostage rescue mission in Iran, Skylab's descent, and the fire at the Titan missile silo in Arkansas.

After working with her on this book about her career as a courtroom illustrator, I concur with Judge Leggett's opinion that she "truly is in a class of her own."

Frank W. Martin
Oak Park, Illinois

Foreword

From the moment television news organizations began covering trials, the courtroom artist was indispensable. Until recent years, cameras were banned from courtrooms. The artist was television's only visual link to the drama generated by the American system of justice. Courtroom artists had to ply their craft under daunting conditions. Up against tight, rigid deadlines, they had to produce drawings that were accurate, clear, and that depicted the most important moments of the trial each day. Finding someone with a fast and artistic hand, a nose for news, and a deadline-resistant iron stomach was very difficult.

Among the few who made the grade, Ida Libby Dengrove was the best. Her full-color drawings not only captured uncanny likenesses of defendants, lawyers, witnesses, jurors, and judges, they also managed to capture the emotion of the moment. Ida's daily torrent of courtroom sketches made our trial coverage come alive on the television screen. Her drawings, sometimes done just minutes before they were aired, were so compelling that notorious villains frequently asked for framed copies after their convictions. In the underworld, being immortalized by Ida Libby Dengrove apparently had a certain perverse cachet.

I continue to be awed by her skills and will always be grateful for the contributions she made to broadcast journalism.

—*Chuck Scarborough*
Anchor, WNBC News 4 New York

358736

Contents

ONE

The First Emmy

THE PHONE AWAKENED ME FROM A DEEP SLEEP AT THREE o'clock in the morning, and I fumbled for the receiver. It was my assignment editor. "Ida, the police have caught the 'Son of Sam,' " she said sharply, "and we want you at the Brooklyn Criminal Court, pronto."

Edith Cahill's voice sparked my adrenaline. The "Son of Sam" had hit the city like a plague, a Jack the Ripper of New York. The killings started on July 29, 1976, and the murderer seemed to favor young, long-haired women. He created such panic that young women were afraid to go out at night for fear of being gunned down. In fact, some women only went out in the evening after putting on a wig or a hat.

This "Son of Sam" killer had murdered three women in the Bronx, two in Queens, and one in Brooklyn. He prowled the streets at night and left strange notes next to his victims.

The city could relax. Since I often worked well past sunset and traveled throughout the metropolitan area, I, too, was relieved that the police had cornered this killer.

I dressed hurriedly and finished my coffee. The train

ride from Allenhurst, New Jersey, to Penn Station in New York City seemed much longer that day than on other mornings when I had sketched controversial people appearing at court hearings. My nervousness had been justified. By the time I caught a cab from the train station to the Brooklyn courthouse, it was surrounded by barricades and uniformed policemen. I knew many of the cops, and I cleared security and entered the courtroom.

It was only eight o'clock, but the courtroom was so crowded that I had a hard time making my way to the front of the room. I immediately pulled out my sketch pad, pencil case, and pastels and looked around the courtroom to get a feel for it. At long last, I was ready for the main event. There were other sketch artists scattered throughout the rows of seats, and we nodded a nervous hello to each other. Uniformed police and plainclothes security people were all over the place.

Suddenly there was considerable movement in front of the judge's bench, and guards escorted an attorney and a heavy-set young man with very curly hair to face the judge. The accused killer seemed to walk without effort. He just floated along. Standing there handcuffed, he was quite ordinary-looking. He wore blue jeans and a pale, blue-striped shirt open at the neck, which exposed a white undershirt.

But the one thing that struck me was his eyes. They didn't seem to focus on anything. They were large and light blue, with a streak of black in the pupil. His eyebrows knitted together in the middle of his forehead, and he had an ever-so-slight smile. That smile and the way his brows framed those peculiar eyes made a frightening image in my mind.

Sketching feverishly, I looked across the courtroom several times. David R. Berkowitz had captured all those present. They sat or stood still, staring at the man who was charged with the murder of twenty-year-old Stacy Moskowitz and the attempted murder of her boyfriend Robert Violante.

Berkowitz told the judge that he lived in suburban Yonkers and worked as a postal clerk. He claimed that demons took possession of him and forced him to prey on young, attractive women. In a clear and even voice, Berkowitz said that he was guilty of killing six women and responsible for blowing the eye out of the head of one man.

Bob Hager, my reporter for the story, tapped me on the shoulder and said that we should get back to the RCA Building, where NBC has its New York headquarters and where I could touch up my sketches. Although it lasted only sixteen minutes, the arraignment had been upsetting, and I was shaky when we left the courtroom. I settled down during the ride to Rockefeller Center but grabbed a bottle of Coca-Cola to revive me. Since I had been up so early and gone without breakfast or lunch, I was running out of steam and ended up exhausted by the time I got home. But my mind focused on the frightening face I had sketched in court. I couldn't get rid of the image.

THE ARRAIGNMENT OF BERKOWITZ WAS ON ONLY THE FIRST of many days I spent on the case as it developed over the next year. Each hearing brought another bizarre or unexpected development.

About a week after the arraignment, NBC News asked me to stay overnight at the St. Regis Hotel in New York so I would be closer to the courtroom. As I had learned many years before, working as a sketch artist for a television network was not a nine-to-five proposition. I called my husband and told him I wouldn't be home that night. The next morning my reporter picked me up at the hotel at seven and drove us to Brooklyn Supreme Court, which is near the Brooklyn Bridge. We approached the square-shaped concrete building, and I saw mobs of people everywhere.

As we tried to make our way to the entrance, a motorcade comprised of a patrol car, two detective squad cars, a white police van, a green van, and three more patrol cars—all with sirens blaring—pulled up to the courthouse. You would have thought that an important dignitary from a foreign country had arrived and that we were protecting him from assassination.

But the fact that the "Son of Sam," an admitted killer, was being so heavily protected didn't please me. I felt it was unfair to the taxpayers of New York City to shoulder the expense of such extensive security.

It was a chore to get inside the courthouse. When people spilled out of the elevator onto the seventh floor, we waited in line to go through security. Police officers manned two magnetometers, the metal-detecting devices used at airports. Everyone submitted to a body search, and, of course, the police went through my portfolio.

Policemen and court officials jammed corridors, but the courtroom was a mess. It held about 250 people, and I don't think there were any spectators in the place. Everyone seemed to be a newspaper, magazine, radio, or television reporter. Or a sketch artist.

When Berkowitz came into the room, fifteen policemen accompanied him, and about half of them surrounded the defendant's table. I guessed that there were several detectives in the crowd keeping an eye out for anyone who might make an attempt on the life of the "Son of Sam."

The crowd crammed themselves into the bench seats so tightly that I felt the sweat of the people next to me. Thank God I had brought a small pad, because I probably could not have found the room for a big one and still been able to sketch; I even kept my pastels on the pad because I had no room to place them beside me.

A special grand jury had been convened and an indictment had been returned against Berkowitz. Justice Leonard E. Yoswein presided over the hearing in which the "Son of Sam" was charged with murdering Stacy Moskowitz and with assaulting her boyfriend Robert Violante, who had lost an eye in the shooting from a .44-caliber bullet. Berkowitz also was charged with criminal possession of a firearm, a snub-nosed bulldog revolver.

Berkowitz, who wore the same clothes he had on during his arraignment, stared straight ahead. Although his eyes had a spooky and spaced-out look, he answered the judge's questions quietly and coherently. After the charges were read to Berkowitz, the judge determined that he was represented by proper counsel and sent the twenty-four-year-old defendant to Kings County Hospital in Brooklyn for psychiatric evaluation.

Then the proceeding ended abruptly. That, I learned long before, was part of the news business. You hurried like there was no tomorrow to the scene, waited around for the players to appear, worked intensely because you never knew how long you'd have access to them, and then started the same routine all over again on the next assignment. The adrenaline kept you going.

My sketches appeared on the network news that night. When I sat in front of the television set at home, the report mesmerized me because it was difficult for me to *see* the defendant when I worked so quickly.

The only thing I could think of when I saw the sketches was the eyes of the "Son of Sam." I kept saying to my husband, "Those are his eyes, those really are his eyes." I realized that this killer was totally out of it; he wasn't in the same world with the rest of us.

My next Berkowitz assignment brought a comic turn. The judge began the session by addressing the district attorney and defense attorneys before Berkowitz was brought into the courtroom. An administrative justice had realized that the defendant was missing, and the proceeding came to a halt until Berkowitz was escorted into the courtroom. This time, though, he wore a gray suit and pale blue shirt because he thought that he had not been properly dressed for his earlier court appearances. One of his attorneys had purchased a new set of clothes for the "Son of Sam."

The judge read a report from two psychiatrists who had examined Berkowitz. Although they found him incapacitated as a result of mental illness and unable to understand the proceedings against him, the judge sent Berkowitz back to the hospital for another battery of tests for both the defense and the prosecution.

As I left the courtroom that day, I heard Eugene Gold, the district attorney, say that the defendant was capable of standing trial and that psychiatry was fundamentally an art and not a science. "The ultimate decision will be made by the court," he predicted.

A strange thing happened to me a few hours later, when I was touching up my sketches in the studio. Haunted by the grotesque look on Berkowitz's face, I realized that some lives are not worth living. That was a dramatic realization for me because I had never believed in capital punishment. But then, with all the effort being made to determine whether Berkowitz was fit to stand trial, the fact was that he might not be tried in a court of law even though he had admitted killing six people and wounding another. To me, he had somehow or in some way been programmed to kill. After seeing and sketching Berkowitz, it seemed to me that this life should not continue.

The next hearing, which was closed to the public, took place in the "secure" dayroom at Kings County Hospital. This time Berkowitz was clad in baggy pajamas and an ill-fitting blue seersucker robe. The hearing lasted two days and addressed the sanity issue. I couldn't help but think about the case of George Metesky, the "mad bomber" who had terrorized New York City in the 1950s. He had been declared incompetent to stand trial and sent in 1957 to Matteawan State Hospital for the Criminally Insane. However, sixteen years later I had covered Metesky's release. I prayed that David Berkowitz would never be allowed out of jail.

In October I sketched the "Son of Sam" again in Kings County Hospital, and this time we heard some horrifying tape recordings of Berkowitz talking to Dr. Daniel Schwartz, the director of forensic psychiatry at the hospital.

"I had nothing against these victims," Berkowitz said. "Who were these people to me? They were just people. Sam made me do it! Through me, he did it for blood. He practically tortured me, tormented me. I'm too human, I have too much love for people. They forced me, but my heart was not really in it. I want people to see David Berkowitz, a nice guy, a loving person. I'm not a bad person."

Because the tapes were mind-boggling and because the room was packed with press people, I found it difficult to sketch that day. Berkowitz looked different, too. He had lost a great deal of weight, wore his new suit, and carried a Bible. Dr. Schwartz testified that Berkowitz was emotionally dead and therefore not capable of defending himself in a trial.

However, the psychiatrist for the prosecution, Dr. David Abrahamsen, had also evaluated Berkowitz and found him competent to stand trial. In a dramatic cross-examination of Dr. Schwartz, Kings County District Attorney Eugene Gold noted that his report showed that the defendant was not emotionally dead, that he showed love, anger, hatred, and compassion. Dr. Schwartz looked at Gold and said that those emotions were short-lived. Berkowitz, meanwhile, stared out into space. Once, though, he did turn to reporters. His eyes lit up, and he looked like a choirboy. Yes, he looked that decent and angelic. Then he adjusted his shirt collar and went back to a zombielike state.

Judge John Starkey ruled that Berkowitz had a working relationship with his attorneys and could listen to their advice. "There may be a question whether he can take advice," the judge said, "but that does not affect his ability to listen. He is a man of positive thoughts and can stand the stress of trial."

I thought that the question of whether the "Son of Sam" would stand trial had been settled, but there was yet another competency hearing, in April 1978. This time the grizzliness of the "Son of Sam" murders came through in testimony. Dr. Schwartz of Kings County Hospital told the court that the defendant said he was possessed by howling demons who had sex with the souls of the victims and that Berkowitz had been promised the same privilege with Donna Lauria, the first victim, whom he murdered on July 29, 1976. But the demons didn't keep their promise to the "Son of Sam."

The Berkowitz case started to come to a conclusion in May 1978. He was questioned separately by three judges—one from Brooklyn, one from Queens, and one from the Bronx. The judges were again concerned about his sanity and about his ability to understand the proceedings. Wearing a blue suit and pin-striped shirt, Berkowitz stated that he was an excellent shot and admitted to all the murders claimed by the "Son of Sam" as well as other crimes connected with the shootings.

The parents of Donna Lauria wept when Berkowitz admitted that he shot their daughter at close range. During a recess, Donna's father erupted. "Justice is not going to be done!" he said. "He should go to the [electric] chair like he is supposed to!"

I didn't know why people expected anything but a hideous end to the "Son of Sam" case. During a sentencing hearing on May 23, guards brought Berkowitz into the courtroom. He rolled his eyes in a monstrous way and contorted his face into grotesque expressions. With his arms flailing in an attempt to get away from the guards, he shouted obscenities at Mrs. Moskowitz, the mother of the last victim.

"Stacy was a whore!" Berkowitz yelled. Mrs. Moskowitz couldn't take it. "You animal! You animal!" she screamed back.

"That's right, that's right, I'll kill her again!" Berkowitz bellowed. He looked and acted like a madman, a monster who didn't belong among rational people.

It was horrible, just horrible. But the ugliness got worse. Berkowitz's outburst hit raw nerves and launched a series of verbal assaults. Robert Violante, the twenty-one-year-old man whom Berkowitz had wounded, suddenly screamed, "You should get killed, you creep!" Then he sank into his seat and sobbed.

As the judge read into the record his belief that Berkowitz had planned the outburst well in advance of the hearing, another man stood up and began to shake with anger. "In the meantime, what about the families?" he shouted. "How can they take this anymore? They are human."

The judge ordered the man out of the courtroom, and I heard him warn police officers. "Don't touch me!" he yelled. "I'll go out on my own!"

Mrs. Moskowitz, shaking like a leaf, suddenly left the courtroom. "Thank God my husband and daughter didn't come today," she said upon her return to the hearing. "They couldn't have taken this."

I, too, was filled with rage as the judge postponed the sentencing. The families of the victims sat and wept. I had never seen nor felt such anger from a defendant. The violence in his eyes scorched each of us in that courtroom.

I'm not sure how I did it, but I managed to do several sketches of Berkowitz. Violante, disfigured physically and emotionally for life, was comforted by his father, and I sketched them—a father placing an arm around his son.

The case came to a close on June 13, 1978, when Berkowitz, undoubtedly sedated into a submissive state, was sentenced to six twenty-five-years-to-life terms. Judge William Kapelman, one of the three city judges who pronounced the sentence, said, "It is my earnest wish that this defendant be imprisoned for the rest of his natural life and until he shall die."

But everyone knew that the "Son of Sam" probably would remain in jail for a maximum of thirty years. He could be imprisoned for most of only one lifetime. That hardly seemed adequate punishment for a diabolical killer.

As Berkowitz was ushered out of the courtroom, a friend of the Moskowitz family, Daniel Carrique, left his seat, growled with deep emotion, and lunged for the defendant. Carrique was apprehended by court guards. Then Berkowitz, a man who had terrorized New York City and had caused such pain, disappeared under heavy guard.

I, along with most New Yorkers, would never forget the "Son of Sam" case. It also had a profound professional impact on me. Throughout the trial I received numerous letters of appreciation from our news directors and producers for capturing the scene and emotion of the case. Because all cameras were prohibited in the courtroom, the Associated Press sent my sketches around the world by wire, and a few of them ended up on the front page of *The New York Times.* That was quite a compliment, because other courtroom illustrators had covered the trial, too.

The greatest compliment to my work came from the New York chapter of the National Academy of Television Arts and Sciences, when it voted me an Emmy Award for Outstanding Individual Craft in the Spot News Category for the sketches I produced on the day David Berkowitz went berserk in the courtroom.

I was very proud when former New York mayor John Lindsay handed me the award in front of my television colleagues and my artistic peers. Over the years I had realized the power and the magic that television brought to the world, and my work was recognized as an important part of television news.

But personally, the trial of David R. Berkowitz had a lasting effect. It convinced me that in rare instances capital punishment is society's only protection against a monstrous form of life, a human who is incapable of human emotions.

TWO

Sketching on Deadline

As odd as it may seem to some people, especially dedicated artists who have poured days and weeks into a single portrait, I never had a difficult time adjusting to the pressure of having just ten or fifteen minutes to complete a sketch that would be aired on WNBC or the "NBC Nightly News." I utilized and refined my experience from previous sketching adventures, which was the best training and apprenticeship an artist could imagine for that kind of work.

I did not plan it that way. It just happened. Life in this country was very different in the 1920s and 1930s, when I grew up in Philadelphia. Most people in those days—including my family—did not have a great deal of material possessions or much money for leisure activities. My twin sister, Freda and I were the second and third youngest of seven children, and my mother always was trying to keep us busy. She often gave us paper, pencils, and crayons to draw or to make copies of pictures. Once, when I was four, she even told me she would hang one drawing on the wall if I completed it. That gave me naughty ideas because I thought if my drawing could hang on the wall then I could draw on walls, too.

Mother never objected but followed me around with her mop and bucket and washed up after me. She encouraged me to draw whenever I wanted to, and my father was equally supportive. One of the most vivid memories of my childhood was the Leibovitz Olympics. It was Papa Leibovitz's ingenious method of encouraging seven children to pursue the arts on an otherwise uneventful Sunday afternoon. The grand prize for the best artistic endeavor was five cents in cash. The competition was fierce. Isadore, fourteen, wrote stories; William, eleven, played violin; Esther, nine, sang psalms; Dora, seven, wrote jingles; Freda and I sketched; Louis, three, scribbled; Papa, who had studied sculpturing when he first arrived in this country from Odessa, sculpted; and Mama embroidered. Somehow the sketches that Freda and I did always won the grand prize.

From that point on, there was no stopping the Leibovitz twins. Our work made quite an impression on the city, and the *Philadelphia Record* ran a front-page article in 1937 about the talented twins. Because our family did not have much money, we had a hard time finding paint supplies. When canvas was not available, we used the nearest things on hand: window shades, kitchen towels, backs of chairs. Even the wallpaper took a beating. Mama Leibovitz, who was forced to rescue her best towels from the bathroom, didn't save the walls from our drawings.

After we started school, our artistic activities increased. When we came home, we found willing models in our parents and then pressed neighbors into service. But our real training in portraiture came when we would get out in real-life surroundings. Once a week we walked to Broad Street Station and sketched people waiting for trains. We also visited the waterfront and found some very willing subjects.

Throughout our early school years our mother went to Atlantic City to work in the summer, and Freda and I accompanied her and sketched portraits on the beach to earn extra money. In fact, we became self-supporting at twelve. By then we were spending our summers in Cape May, New Jersey, where I drew portraits for a fee. I bought clothes, art materials, and many things for myself, which relieved my parents of the responsibility, since they had so many other mouths to feed.

Working on the beach at Cape May was one of the most enriching experiences of my life and probably gave me the best preparation for the work I later did for NBC. I sketched so many different faces of such a variety of people. Sometimes I even drew their pets—cats, dogs, birds, even horses. I charged a dollar to sketch a person and two dollars for an animal because the animal did not stay still.

In some ways it was amazing that I survived the summers. Because the mosquitoes were so vicious, I kept myself covered with jackets, long-sleeved blouses with high collars, kerchiefs, and pants, but those creatures still got me.

The other problem was the wind, especially at night, and I worked hard to keep all my art materials together. At eighty-five pounds I thought I would have to strap myself to the easel on blustery nights. But I met such a variety of people and learned to work quickly. That experience paid off handsomely decades later.

Believe it or not, Eastman Kodak Company also influenced my life. In 1930, when I was twelve, the company ran a promotion that entitled every child my age to receive a Brownie box camera for nothing. With the help of my brothers, I bought film and took the first photographs of my life. I realized the great depth that the camera was able to provide in photographs. But I thought that if the camera could capture images mechanically, my eyes could do better. My eyes caught human emotion. Since I was living and breathing, I felt I could provide a different kind of depth in my art.

I entered my work in local, national, and international

art competitions, and suddenly my world was a very happy one, indeed. I won a goodly number of awards and scholarships, and those fueled my drive, my dream to be a good artist. While I still was in high school, the National Youth Administration provided great artistic encouragement as well as a stipend of twenty dollars per month for teaching adult art classes at a local school. In those Depression-era days, I was grateful for every opportunity to advance my art and to earn money.

Upon high school graduation, I received a Philadelphia Board of Education scholarship. I chose Moore College of Art, which had been incorporated into the old Philadelphia School of Design for Women, the oldest women's art school in the country.

There, one of my instructors, Arthur Meltzer, opened my eyes to light and shadow, an artist's way of seeing dimensional form, proportion, and perspective. He taught me the necessity of doing a thumbnail sketch, showing composition and light contrasts, before working on a major illustration. I later utilized those lessons on almost every sketch I completed in the courtroom.

During my sophomore year, two incidental events happened to me that would later shape my career. Freda, who also attended Moore College, and I sometimes stopped after our classes at city hall to meet my brother. He worked in the building. Being a curious woman, I sat through a few court cases, and a whole new world opened up for me because most people sat still and were easy to sketch. There also were lovely architectural carvings to capture in each room. Then, of course, my eye turned to the attorneys in action. The whole scene was so different from sketching in train and bus stations or on the beach.

I also sketched historical scenes throughout Philadelphia for the city newspapers. I did it on a free-lance basis, which gave me a new forum for my work as well as extra money for college. Ever since then I have displayed a considerable amount of my work through the mass media.

The action of the courtroom attracted me during my senior year in college. Each student was required to hang illustrations on one wall in the school for competition in the John Frederick Lewis Memorial Fellowship, a postgraduate fund for European travel and art study. One of my best sketches was of Judge Lewis, who presided over the Philadelphia hearings in the infamous Murder, Inc. trials of 1938–40. Covering the trial was both intriguing and frightening for me. I had been naturally drawn to the drama of the courtroom, and Murder, Inc., a group that assassinated people for the crime syndicate, fueled my interest in the criminal justice system.

In a ten-year period, organized crime ordered and contracted for approximately one thousand murders to sustain its rackets. The victims were shot, strangled with a rope, stabbed with an ice pick, or thrown into quicklime pits.

The names tossed around in court were well known: Bugsy Siegel, Meyer Lansky, Frank Costello, Lucky Luciano, Dutch Schultz, Vito Genovese, Joey Adonis, and Albert Anastasia. I also remembered a man named Harry Strauss because he was accused of killing thirty men in twelve cities.

What I saw and what I drew during the Murder, Inc., cases gave me a framework to use in all the other organized-crime trials I later did for NBC.

I also "discovered" men during my senior year in college and found lawyers at the courthouse, in particular, attractive and quite handsome men. I enjoyed discussing cases with them, and they showed great interest in my sketches.

But I won the traveling fellowship after graduation and temporarily lost romantic interest in lawyers. The Second World War had already started in Europe, so I wrote the board of governors that I would do my foreign study in Mexico. What I did not tell them was that I was going to use the six-hundred-dollar grant to cover expenses for both my twin sister and me. We spent six glorious months traveling and sketching our way through Mexico City, Xochimilco, Taxco, Cuernavaca, and Acapulco. We came back with a slew of paintings that were shown at the Carlen Galleries. The exhibit received excellent reviews and earned a story in *Time* magazine.

I moved into a free-lance illustrating job at the *Philadelphia Bulletin,* where I did many sketches of the new recruits at Camp Dix. That's how I met my husband, Dr. Edward Dengrove, a physician with a private's rank stationed at Camp Dix and waiting for his officer's commission. He watched me sketch, walked over to me, and invited me to lunch.

My God, those were trying times. The war in Europe dominated the news, and most people knew that sooner or later the United States would be involved in the conflict. I did advertising and commercial art work, taught art classes, and produced maps for the Works Progress Administration. On top of that, I fell in love and married Captain Edward Dengrove, who had been assigned to the Army Air Force at Morrison Field in West Palm Beach, Florida.

Our dream of a quiet life together blew apart one Sunday when we were in the car on the way back from one of our long walks along the shore of Lake Worth and heard about the attack on Pearl Harbor. Just before Christmas, Ed learned that he was going overseas, and I found myself back in Philadelphia teaching art classes in the public school system.

That did not last too long. I did a short stint illustrating a pilot's manual for a local company and accepted a job with the USO Camp Show to visit hospitals and to sketch amputees whose parents could not visit them until after they were fitted with the proper limbs. It was tough duty. There were many sad cases. Many of our boys had both limbs missing, some were burned beyond recognition, and others died the day after I had sketched them.

Ed, fortunately, was not one of the patients. Although he ended up as a base and flight surgeon for General Chennault and the 14th Air Force (the Flying Tigers) in China, he returned home safely, and we settled in Monmouth County, New Jersey, where we raised our family. By 1949 we had two boys, Richard and Robert, but motherhood did not keep me from my artwork and from art exhibits. I continued my USO Camp Show work, and in November 1949 found out that domesticity had not dampened my "instant portraiture" skills.

On a trip sponsored by the League of Women Voters to the United Nations in New York, I obtained special permission to sketch a Security Council meeting and even gained access to the delegates' lounge. However, I was told that Soviet foreign minister Andrei Vishinsky did not care to be sketched. But on that day, he gave a fiery speech denying a U.N. report that two Eastern Bloc countries—Albania and Bulgaria—had been supplying arms to guerrillas in Greece.

I could not help myself and just sketched like mad to capture the scene. The *Asbury Park Press* used them in a story about the league's trip to the United Nations and ran a separate story about me. The newsmen who had covered our trip said I had the ability to work fast and produced startlingly accurate likenesses of people.

During the next twenty-three years I raised my children and refined my art skills at every opportunity. I taught art classes in the basement of our house, accepted portrait commissions, exhibited my work at the state museum in Trenton and other local galleries, and illustrated a book. During our family vacations, I also visited practically every art museum in Europe, including the Eastern Bloc countries.

I thought it was extremely important for an artist to build on the past, to know great art, to study the masters, to understand techniques. So during the 1950s and 1960s I studied every aspect of art and worked in everything from landscapes to still lifes. I did watercolors, oils, prints, etchings, lithographs, drypoints, and silk screen printing. And drawings.

I thought that the idea of my art was to express human emotions on the canvas. My work was not abstract. I drew whatever I saw and whatever I felt from people.

MY TWIN SISTER, WHO WORKED FOR ABC AS AN ARTIST, was an integral part of a news organization. I also remembered the excitement and fun of sketching at the United Nations and recalled the flattering comments the press made about my work so many years before.

With that in mind, I picked up the phone, called up Bernard Schussman, the news director at WNBC in New York City, and made an appointment for the next day. When I arrived for the interview, he was busy, and his secretary asked me to wait for ten minutes. So I pulled out my sketchpad and pencils and completed a portrait of her. As she escorted me into Schussman's office, I showed it to her. I'll never forget her words. "You just did that?" she said. Then the woman presented both me and the sketch to Schussman, and I was hired on the spot.

The assignment desk called the next day and asked me to be at Supreme Court on Centre Street in New York to cover a hearing about a controversy that writer Clifford Irving and his wife had gotten themselves into. I teamed up with another "rookie," a woman named Pat Collins, but the Irvings did not appear in the courtroom. Instead, I sketched the lawyer and the courtroom scene. During a recess, the judge requested that I join him in his chambers. "May I see your sketches?" he asked. I didn't know what he wanted or was going to do with my sketches. Finally he said, "They are excellent, and we have a few minutes. Would you touch up my face? I'd be delighted to sit and pose for you."

It was a marvelous opportunity to get an extra sketch

for the station, and I even managed to start a close-up of his head. The judge—and more importantly the station producers—liked the sketches, and Pat and I were informed that our story would be aired that evening. I got home just in time for the show and saw the sketches followed with my byline in good-sized letters.

What a rush! I suddenly realized that the television screen was the best art gallery in the world to exhibit my work. Millions of people could see my sketches. Working in television opened up a whole new door, another phase of my art.

But some of the excitement of my new job wore off quickly because of the daily commuting grind. It was not easy. The trip by train took one and three-quarters hours from Allenhurst to Penn Station, and the trains in 1972 were in shabby condition. Windows and doors did not work properly. The toilets were foul-smelling and very dirty. In the winter the heating systems were unbelievably poor. It was either too hot or too cold. You literally suffered through the trip. The trains were forever late, and I never returned home to the Jersey Shore on time.

There always was a male chauvinist or two on the train, too. They sat down next to you and said, "Do you work in the city? If I had a wife like you, I'd never let her work in the city." Early on, I also learned never to take my raincoat off and place it on the overhead rack because it probably would not be there by the time I reached New York City.

A typical day for me actually began the night before, when I picked out my wardrobe and put together my drawing pencils, my pastels, and my sketchbooks. I got up at five or six o'clock the next morning, ate a light breakfast, and never took more than a half hour to get myself together. It was a discipline with me, and I never missed a train. My husband drove me to the Allenhurst station for the 6:03 or the 7:03 train, depending on where in the city a trial was held and how early it began.

If on the previous day I had not been told what trial I would cover, I called the assignment desk as soon as I hit New York City. I had to hurry to make some trials because there never seemed to be a cab outside Penn Station. The best thing to do was to walk a block or two to the right or left of the station. I thought the better bet was to go left, but sometimes lost and ended up on the subway.

In 1979, after I had become a seasoned commuter and news-sensitive illustrator, I compiled my own list of different courthouse news offices and asked the officers in charge what was going on in their courtrooms. I then made a list and presented it to the assignment editor, who frequently sent me to one of those trials. Often I was the first—or only—newsperson on the scene.

That probably was the single most important factor for a courtroom illustrator. Having a good seat had a great deal to do with the success of your sketch and your point of view. There didn't seem to be a lot of competition among illustrators during my early years with NBC, but that situation certainly changed as more and more illustrators found their way into the courtroom.

Many of the other artists were nice, but some were just plain hostile. One time, an illustrator literally attacked me with her portfolio because I was first in line to clear security at a trial. Another time the same woman was furious with me because I had finished a sketch of a witness who testified for just a few minutes, and she had not yet completed hers.

OVER THE YEARS, PEOPLE FREQUENTLY ASKED ME HOW I WAS able to create sketches so quickly and get everything into them, including the court atmosphere. My success, in part, was based on years of practice and a healthy respect for the fundamentals of art. Like any other craft, hard work also was an important ingredient. But the technical and logistical preparation for each day and each trial meant a great deal, too.

Since I am a small woman, I found it difficult to carry anything overly large or heavy. I was forever getting in and out of cabs and trains, so it was doubly important for me not to carry a large assortment of art supplies. I carried just one small metal box that contained Nupastels (hard pastels), which I could break down into smaller pieces—the yellows, the oranges, the reds, the purples, the blues, the greens, the browns, the grays, the blacks, and, of course, white. I also used Othello pastel pencils, especially those with a skin tone; carbon pencils; and a black, fine-line Mont Blanc pen.

The sizes of my sketchbooks varied. I started out with a fourteen-by-seventeen-inch book and progressed to a fifteen-by-nineteen. I tried to keep the sketchbooks small because of the limited space in the courtroom. Most artists, however, used a twenty-four-by-thirty pad.

The one thing I immediately became accustomed to in working in the courtroom was dirty clothes and huge cleaning bills. Because I was unable to wear plastic gloves while sketching, my hands and the rest of me generally were spotted with pastels and pencil smudges. Once I started to work, I didn't think much about getting dirty. But I was always amused by the fact that when I finished a drawing I tried to clean *it* up and didn't worry about my hands, face, and clothes.

As I've already said, getting a good seat in the courtroom was extremely important. Throughout my fifteen years in television news, the reporters often gave up their front-row seats at spectacular trials to me. Many times I started my sketch with a perspective of the courtroom. I drew my horizon line, my point of infinity, and then the defendant's table, the jury box, the judge's bench, and the witness box.

Sometimes there seemed to be a cast of thousands during a hearing, and that was very frustrating for me because I was one of the few illustrators who tried to get everyone into a sketch. I also listened closely to the proceedings because I wanted to get a feeling for the legal maneuvering, and then turned my attention to the defendant to see if there was guilt or innocence in his eyes. The guilt or the innocence always showed in the eyes. To me, the eyes were the windows of the soul. I was amazed at the different emotions I felt from defendants and always tried to portray accurately that feeling in my sketches through their eyes.

Sometimes the jury was a rather interesting group of people, and I attempted to show differences among them—their attitudes, their expressions. I always wanted our television viewers to feel what was going on. After sketching the jury, for example, I regularly predicted that a decision had been reached. I'd tell my reporter, "Get ready because I think that a verdict is coming." And when I covered a trial by myself, I'd call the assignment desk and ask that they send a camera crew to the courthouse when I felt a verdict was about to be rendered. Fortunately, I rarely misread the jury.

Although a byline accompanied my sketches when aired on WNBC or the network news, my work was made possible through good, old-fashioned teamwork. The reporters were hardworking and creative as well as resourceful and clever. They knew their stories and asked the right questions. Many times they spoke to me about what I should look for in the courtroom. As we got to know each other, I anticipated their approach to a story and what they would say on the air. It was important for me to know how the reporters worked and important for them to know how I worked. They gave their all to an assignment, and I tried to do the same.

It also was important to give them the time and the space they needed to complete their part of the assignment. Bob Teague, who later became an anchorman at WNBC, was the ultimate professional to work with and assisted me whenever he could. And since he usually had a film crew with him, I rode back to the studio with them when we worked a story together. I quickly learned to be quiet as we rode together because Bob would either think through the trial and figure out what to put in his report or just relax and even doze off for a few minutes before hitting the studio and all the deadline craziness.

And things always were crazy. People didn't stop and talk to you unless it pertained to a story. During my early years, I didn't have my own desk in the newsroom, so I just settled at any empty desk and stayed out of the way. I always waited until the story—at least from my end—was okay. A nod from the producer at the end of the day meant that no cleanup or changes were needed in my sketches and that I could head home.

In some cases, though, I was just beside myself the way my sketches were handled after they left my hands. Producers sometimes sent motorcycle couriers to me at a courthouse when we were on a tight deadline, and I watched them roll up the sketches and place them in a tube. That aggravated me because I knew that it was difficult to unroll sketches and keep them flat once they arrived back at the studio to be photographed. It was plain silly for me to get upset about such a little thing, but there was nothing I could suggest, since I had never seen a courier holding a large portfolio on a motorcycle.

When I first started sketching for television, I felt considerable pressure and rushed through arraignments because I thought I should have several sketches—not just one—of the scene. Since they lasted only five or ten minutes, I completed the sketches by re-creating the courtroom scene from memory after the hearing.

That experience paid off for me when I was asked to cover trials in New Jersey. Many courts in the state didn't allow artists to sketch at all, so I observed, took notes, and left the courtroom to re-create everything I saw. No one ever complained about the quality or depictions of those sketches.

One time, however, I ended up smack in the middle

of a major legal controversy concerning the Supreme Court of New Jersey and NBC. I was sketching a trial in Hackensack, New Jersey, that involved a ménage à trois with a doctor, his wife, and his mistress. They were accused of molesting and assaulting the mistress's nine-year-old son. During the morning recess, the judge invited me into his chambers, asked for my sketches, and then folded them up. He literally ruined them and informed us that his act was justified under the Canons of Judicial Ethics, which provided that "the making of sketches of the court or of any person in it during sessions of the court or recesses between sessions . . . are calculated to detract from the essential dignity of the proceedings, degrade the court, and create misconceptions with respect thereto in the mind of the public and should not be permitted."

My reporter, Jim Collins, immediately contacted the network. I later appeared with network attorneys in the Supreme Court of New Jersey, where NBC argued its right to have me sketch the trial. CBS submitted a brief in support of our case, and an attorney for the New Jersey Bar Association argued our cause *amicus curiae.*

NBC stated that an effective manner of reporting judicial proceedings includes the use of sketches, prepared in court, constituting pictorial representation of the courtroom scene. It was suggested that the use of sketches during a televised news broadcast imparts an immediacy and a realism not otherwise to be had.

The court didn't address NBC's contention that it had a constitutional right to sketch trials, but it ruled in our favor. "A judge must always maintain decorum in courtroom during the course of a trial or any other judicial proceeding," wrote the Supreme Court of New Jersey. "It was presumably to preserve this dignity that the prohibition upon sketching was originally adopted. We are assured by the broadcasting companies that the proposed sketching will be unobtrusive and will not distract the attention of witnesses or jurors, nor be in any way a coercive influence upon them. We see no reason to doubt this assurance and note that today such sketching is permitted in most courts throughout the country."

Needless to say, I was elated with amending the judicial proceedings in the state. Whoever would have believed that a nonjournalist—an artist, a teacher, a mother—would have such an impact on the way trials were covered in New Jersey. I was very proud of my role and the fact that I opened the court for all artists in New Jersey. From that point on it was such a relief to sketch in court and not worry about taking notes and doing sketches from memory.

However, I was not always fortunate to have such a supportive reporter as Jim Collins. Sometimes the television newsroom was like a revolving door, and reporters just didn't last too long. One was our answer to Geraldo Rivera, who worked at ABC. The new reporter covered the John Wayne Wilson trial with me. Wilson had been accused of killing Roseanne Quinn, a teacher who worked with the deaf, and the case later became the subject of a book and movie called *Looking for Mr. Goodbar.* After being arraigned, Wilson pleaded insanity and the reporter said, "Don't bother finishing the sketch; we're not going on the air with the story." After the arraignment, Wilson committed suicide in his jail cell.

In other cases, I covered trials without a reporter. That became fun and challenging because I played two roles. I would sketch, take notes, and make sure I got certain facts as well as the right names of the defendants, attorneys, and judges. I sometimes wished I could write with my toes because I had to draw with my fingers. It was difficult, but I managed to come through for the news department. My work, especially in my early days in television, was appreciated, too. A producer told me, "You know, Ida, if there were a fire and we didn't have a camera crew, I think they'd send you to cover it."

The most difficult aspect of working in television news

was covering three or four trials per day or working for WNBC and the "NBC Nightly News" at the same time. The pressure of covering and sketching that many trials was enough to cope with. Then I adjusted to multiples—two reporters, two producers, two camera crews, two whatevers.

Because of deadline pressure I often didn't have time to clean up the sketches. I just rushed out of the courtroom and sent them back to the studio or gave them to the film crew.

Having good cameramen in the studio or in the field was extremely important to my work and to the overall story presentation during the newscast. At times, though, when I first began sketching for television, the camera people had to feel their way through about how best to shoot my illustrations. Often they used an enhancer on the camera lens, which was used to fade out some details. On the contrary, I thought that every detail should be shown.

At other times, camera crews really impressed me with their creative ability and with their ever-growing technical capability. Once, Carl Stern, a reporter who came up from the Washington bureau for a story we were working on, said, "Ida, we're going live." I didn't know what he meant by that. He then told me that we had a minicam near the courthouse, and my work would be pasted to the side of the truck and beamed live over the airwaves as part of the lead story right into television sets.

Well, since I had been born shortly after the end of the First World War, I was just flabbergasted. As the cameraperson photographed my sketches, I watched the nightly news program live on a monitor. For me, that was something right out of Buck Rogers! Although I didn't have time to clean up or touch up the sketches, they looked good even when photographed and transmitted with this new technology. I always felt a great camaraderie with cameramen. They were all warm, friendly, and artistically driven. They appreciated my work, and I certainly appreciated theirs. They were an important part of my courtroom illustration career and literally made me look good.

In another respect, I was glad to know that camera crews were outside of the courtroom ready to photograph my sketches because of a very selfish reason. Since I have always been a perfectionist, I had a tendency to linger on and on with a sketch. But you could overwork a drawing and take the spontaneity—the life—out of it. It can get too hard-looking instead of fresh and free. With a camera crew waiting in the hallway or outside the building, I avoided that dilemma.

All of us had bad days, too. At times it seemed as if the reporters, cameramen, and the chief illustrator couldn't get anything accomplished for the news directors and producers. You must have a really tough hide to work, to succeed, and to stay in the news business. Unfortunately, I didn't have that kind of toughness. When my pride was hurt, which happened more than once, I cried like a little girl.

I sincerely tried to do my best on every assignment, but there were times when I knocked myself out for the station or the network but my sketches didn't make the evening broadcast. Perhaps my pride was so hurt because I sure wasn't working at NBC for the money. In fact, it was a losing proposition. In my early years I earned one hundred dollars per day. It cost me a minimum of twenty dollars per day for transportation alone. In New York City, meals ran me twenty to thirty dollars per day, and I spent ten or fifteen dollars on art supplies. Then Uncle Sam took approximately forty dollars out of my fee for taxes.

So from time to time, I felt utterly frustrated because I traveled almost five hours per day to and from the city, sketched like a madwoman on deadline, and then had some producer decide not to use my work on the air. The only thing that made me feel worse was when I went out of my way to capture an exclusive scene and then had someone decide against using it.

For example, I covered the trial of Gennadi Zakharov, who was accused of spying for the Soviet Union. I had walked past the informant in the case, a Guyanese student, who was testifying before the grand jury. So I sketched him from memory and called the assignment desk with the information. The editor said, "Oh, that's great." NBC and WNBC, which had first reproduction rights to my sketches, didn't use the sketch, but *The Daily News* wanted it. I was furious. We had exclusive material on a key witness in the case. David Diaz, the reporter, told me he was doing a story on a suspected American spy held in the Soviet Union and not on the Zakharov case.

I couldn't understand the decision, and the news producers became quite irritated with me. But, as the saying goes, that was show business. I packed up and took the next train home.

Unpleasant situations happen in every job. Mine, thankfully, occurred rarely and probably had as much to do with what I expected from myself.

For the fifteen years during which I illustrated the courtroom scenes for WNBC and NBC, I was satisfied, gratified, and excited about my job. I saw and experienced so much, and it was the most exciting period of my life.

THREE

Organized Crime

THE TRIALS OF ORGANIZED CRIME FIGURES WERE ALWAYS media events, and the courtrooms were packed with press people and spectators, all waiting to see Mafia chieftains parade through the place with their high-priced lawyers. It was the best show in town, and many, especially the more controversial or well-known mob figures, overplayed their roles as much for the media as for the jury.

Godfathers usually showed up in expensive and well-tailored suits and smiled a greeting at prosecutors. It was as if they were saying, "Catch me if you can." But when confronted with charges of wrongdoing, these men paradoxically claimed that they didn't know anything about criminal activities because they were honest businessmen. They hadn't victimized anyone but rather were the victims of the government's political harassment and of the prosecutors' frame-up. Godfathers complained that witnesses against them were out-and-out liars or were paid by the government to fabricate stories about them.

Defendants further complicated the proceedings sometimes by claiming that they either didn't speak or didn't understand English, while others played on the sympathy of the jury by claiming that someone in their family was gravely ill. It seemed that every time a grand jury returned an indictment against a reputed Mafia figure, we also discovered "a cancer" had struck the defendant's family. In fact, several defendants said that they had cancer, too.

But once the trial moved beyond public posturing and into testimony from law enforcement officials and from eyewitnesses documenting mob actions, the mood of the proceedings changed from a rehearsal for a television sitcom into a real-life horror show full of blood and death.

The taped phone conversations of those under indictment were filled with obscenities that would make a sailor blush. But worse was the indifference to human life. The description of a killing or multiple killings was bone-chilling, but the originality that mob killers brought to their work shocked the press and the spectators. I never imagined human beings killed in such a variety of ways.

These people also promoted and controlled multimillion-dollar empires that involved every illegal activity imaginable, from importing drugs to running extortion rings and from directing car theft gangs to operating prostitution houses.

The most important of the organized-crime trials took place in 1986. Dubbed the Mob Commission trial after the government's attempt to jail members of mob's national ruling commission, the boss and sometimes underboss of top crime families found themselves in court.

I covered the trial, which lasted ten weeks, and found it absolutely fascinating. The crime family bosses were indicted on charges that they conducted the affairs of the ruling council in a racketeering pattern that included murder, loan sharking, labor payoffs, and extortion in the concrete industry of New York City.

The defendants included Anthony ("Fat Tony") Salerno of the Genovese family; Anthony ("Tony Ducks") Corallo, underboss Salvatore ("Tom Mix") Santoro, and *consigliere* Christopher ("Christie Tick") Furnari of the Lucchese family; Carmine ("The Snake") Persico and underboss Gennaro ("Jerry Lang") Langella of the Columbo family; and acting boss Philip ("Rusty") Rastelli and Capo Anthony ("Bruno") Indelicato, suspected of being involved in the death of fellow mobster Carmen Galente, of the Bonanno family.

The most important pre-Mob Commission trial development made headlines when another defendant, Paul ("Big Paul") Castellano, seventy-three, head of the Gambino family, died in a gangland-style execution in Manhattan outside Sparks Steak House on Forty-sixth Street between Second and Third avenues. Although he was a brother-in-law of the late Carlo Gambino, Castellano and his heir apparent, Thomas Bilotti, were killed by three trench-coated figures using automatic weapons.

Castellano, who was hit six times in the head and body, reportedly "talked too much" to authorities, and it was rumored that John Gotti, another Gambino family member, arranged the assassination both to grab control of the family and to keep more damaging information from falling into the hands of prosecutors.

With a strange array of so-called soldiers accompanying them, the defendants arrived for the trial in packs and marched together through airport-fashion security checkpoints and into the courtroom. The soldiers of each family sat together in the gallery; they were poorly dressed and had very bad body odor. Sometimes, when they sat next to me, the smell was quite sickening. It seemed as if it had been weeks since they had showered or changed clothes. Some men were toothless and hadn't shaved in days, and other soldiers spoke in exceptionally loud voices, as if they were used to being heard above the noise in the street.

They literally seemed to live and exist for their lords, the Godfathers; their peasant look was so strong it seemed as if they could be characters for a medieval Pieter

Brueghel painting. Yet most of the soldiers were nice to me because, I think, they were Italian and were interested in art. They intently watched me as I sketched the events of the trial.

Although each defendant faced multiple twenty-year prison terms, the Godfathers looked at the prosecutors with scorn and at Judge Richard Owen with great indifference. They showed little respect for the court or for law enforcement authorities. You could see the ruthlessness and killer instinct in their eyes, and they acted as if they were beyond reproach.

Carmine Persico, boss of the Columbo family, even conducted his own defense with the aid of attorney Frank Lopez. During one speech made to the jury, Persico called the prosecution's case "a bus trip through tinsel town." He tried to make the court believe that everything said about him was a fabrication and that the testimony against organized crime was a simple fantasy. For me, Persico's role as a court jester and his cartoonlike face brought an interesting dimension to the trial. The courtroom became, at times, a never-never land with Damon Runyon-like figures.

Each day "Fat Tony" Salerno walked into court with a cane in hand and an unlit cigar in his mouth. He had lost a great deal of weight while in jail, and his flesh literally sagged on his body. With heavy, dark circles under his eyes, a puffy face, and poor skin color, Salerno looked more pathetic than menacing. He kept to himself and rarely talked with other mob bosses, but that familiar scorn for the court was ever-present in his eyes.

"Tony Ducks" Corallo, a teddy bear-looking man who had become fond of my sketches and requested several through his lawyer, made the most noise during the trial by constantly tapping the defendant's table with his fingers while listening to testimony.

Throughout the trial I was struck by the stark contrast between the appearance of the defendants and the reality of the testimony. Seated there at the defendants' table together, the Godfathers looked so old and so incapable of the vicious acts attributed to them. The images of these men in the courtroom were so similar to sequences in the movie *The Godfather,* especially those featuring Marlon Brando as Don Corleone.

Although mob bosses paid high fees to top criminal litigators, their attorneys must have found it difficult working on this case because the defendants were so totally in control. The Persico defense was an excellent example; Frank Lopez, the lawyer, appeared to be window dressing to Persico's showboating courtroom antics.

A short partition separated the court from the audience, the families of the defendants, the press and numerous sketch artists, and courtroom buffs who daily tried to gain entrance to the trial. Many people who sat through the entire trial appeared to be from the city's Little Italy, wore black wool stocking hats rolled up on their heads, and spoke loudly in Italian and fractured English.

Although the rendering of the verdict is a tense time in any trial, the moment was especially melodramatic in the Mob Commission case. The forelady, a black woman dressed in a bright red blouse, stood before the court for twenty minutes to read the jury's findings on all the charges. With a tear in her eye, the woman sat down and seemed utterly exhausted. I wondered if the tear represented fear of the defendants or relief that a long trial was about to end.

The jury had rendered an awesome verdict and found the Godfathers guilty as charged. The sentences, handed out in early 1987, were devastating to the aging bosses of organized crime: Salerno, Persico, Langella, Corallo, Santoro, and Furnari received one-hundred-year terms, and Indelicato received a forty-year sentence. With the exception of the powerful Gambino family, the mob leadership in New York City—and the country—had been put behind bars.

No matter how skillful John Gotti, recently proclaimed as organized crime's kingpin and the undisputed leader of the most powerful crime organization in the country, had been in avoiding prosecutors during the Mob Commission trial, he still found himself in court facing a variety of criminal charges. I first sketched him in 1986, when he was accused of assaulting Queens resident Romual Piecyk, who had first appeared in court with an arm in a brace and who had looked as if he had gone through a terrible beating.

But Judge Ann Dufficy delayed the proceedings for several days when Piecyk disappeared. Upon his reappearance, Piecyk failed to identify Gotti and Frank Colletta, also charged in the incident. The judge had no recourse except to dismiss the case, but everyone in the courtroom understood that Piecyk, a man who still was recovering from his injuries, had been threatened during his disappearance with more bodily harm if he chose to testify. Fear jumped out of the man's eyes; he was too jittery to continue the case.

Intimidation, it seemed, became the hallmark of any criminal proceeding against John Gotti. I next saw Gotti a short time later in the Brooklyn federal courthouse when he and six codefendants were charged with taking part in a criminal enterprise that involved loan-sharking, gambling, hijacking, and killing at least three people.

Even jury selection created problems in this case. I honestly believed that most people were afraid to have anything to do with this case and already had read or had heard about Gotti's reputation. If they weren't plain frightened, many prospective jurors stated that they had formed some opinion about the defendants or had known a person related to the defendants. The prosecution faced a formidable task in picking a jury that would evaluate the evidence in the case and render a just verdict.

Gotti, who had been nicknamed Dapper Don for good reason, wore expensive suits—each reportedly cost more than one thousand dollars—and beautiful shirts and silk ties.

Whatever the situation, he carried himself with a certain *joie de vivre.* Even after the judge, upon the recommendation of the prosecutor and a dozen law enforcement officials, had revoked his one-million-dollar bail and sent him to jail for ten months so he wouldn't pressure witnesses or engage in other criminal activity, Gotti shrugged off the setback. The judge had called Gotti "a bold not to say reckless man who can fairly be described as dangerous to other persons and therefore worthy of detention." In fact, he made a fashion statement during his incarceration and added another chapter to his swaggering style.

His prison "fatigues" consisted of a lovely safari shirt and matching pants, and I never—not once—saw a hair out of place. He prided himself on his excellent grooming and took great pleasure in giving some class to the so-called Mafia holding pen at the Metropolitan Correctional Center at Foley Square. The lockup housed Gotti as well as the bosses of the Columbo and Genovese families and Gaetano Badalamenti, charged with operating a heroin ring in what eventually became the infamous Pizza Connection trial.

One time during a morning recess in Gotti's trial, I found myself walking beside the defendant and showed him a sketch I had done of him. He liked it very much, and we started a lengthy conversation about art. I found him quite soft-spoken and exceptionally charming. Once again, though, I had been hit by the great contradiction of appearance versus testimony.

The prosecutor made a statement to the jury that Gotti had murdered men to achieve his place in the Gambino crime family, and then one witness after another with horrible criminal records testified under immunity about the criminal deeds of the Godfather. However, there seemed to be a legal stroke of genius that had originally been planned by the witnesses or by the threat of intimidation on the part of Gotti. On the stand, several key figures stated that the prosecution had bribed or had forced them into making incriminating statements about the defendant.

Right there in front of everyone—prosecutor, judge, jury, and Gotti—they recanted previous recollections of events. The whole proceeding became muddled because you couldn't tell what testimony was true or what was manufactured by the witnesses for their own personal gain in terms of a deal worked out with the prosecution or in terms of avoiding the wrath of Gotti.

I felt an undercurrent of intimidation in the courtroom daily and once experienced it directly on my way home from the trial. As I waited for the elevator, John Carnellia, one of the codefendants, approached me. "I saw you talking to Mr. Gotti," he said menacingly. "Yes," I replied, "and I'm so glad he liked my sketches." "Did you do one of me?" he asked. When I explained that I had also sketched him, Carnellia demanded that I show it to him. He looked at it, stared at me, threw it up in the air, and started to put his hand on me.

After hearing about the criminal acts of these people in court, I became terrified. I didn't know what the man wanted or what he was going to do. We heard some people walking toward us, so I grabbed the sketch off the floor, dashed into the open elevator, and rushed into the street, where I quickly made for a cab. I never acknowledged or spoke to Carnellia or Gotti again.

Later, when the jury came back with a not guilty verdict, I wasn't the least bit surprised. I saw the intimidation on the faces of the jurors when I sketched them throughout the trial, and the sigh of relief about the verdict and about the end of the trial was so obvious as the judge released them from duty.

All the defendants clapped their approval, and Gotti had a Cheshire cat smile on his face. Then they hugged their attorneys and kissed them European-style on each cheek. Although Gotti himself had been in jail for ten months, everyone in court, especially the prosecutors and the media, believed that the incarceration may have saved the Godfather because other mob chieftains had reportedly wanted him out of the way so he couldn't make more inroads into their organized-crime turf. "NBC Nightly News" used nine of my sketches from the last day of the trial, a record for one story.

The Pizza Connection trial provided the world with one of the most insightful views of how the Sicilian Mafia operated, and by extension, how the sister group in the United States managed its criminal activities. This case also represented a high point of cooperation between law enforcement agencies in Italy and the United States in an effort to stem the course of international crime.

The case began in late October 1985 when Tomasso Buscetta, an Italian, testified in New York City against twenty-two former members of the American and Sicilian Mafia who had formed a worldwide, multimillion-dollar drug network and distributed heroin through pizza parlors. Security had been increased because mobsters of two nations were present at the trial and the proceeding itself threatened the viability of the organizations to conduct business as usual.

Buscetta, a muscular man who obviously had had his face reconstructed, was seated between an interpreter and a federal marshal. The interpreter translated everything Buscetta said from Italian to English for the court, and all defendants who didn't speak English wore translation monitors.

Serving as a top aide to Capo di Tutti Capi Gaetano Badalamenti, the boss of all bosses in Sicily, Buscetta had moved to the United States after the Sicilian Mafia had suspended him from their activities for violating their rules of personal conduct. He had been caught smuggling cigarettes without the permission of his superiors and then betrayed his wife by chasing after another woman. In Sicily, that made Buscetta a renegade.

With maps of the Italian mainland and Sicily on the

wall behind him, Buscetta documented Mafia rites and rules that were first revealed by Joseph Valachi in the 1960s. When asked how he became a member of the Mafia, Buscetta said that he had been watched by other members before they asked him to join in a special ceremony. At the secret meeting, he took an oath pledging his total allegiance to the group and was given a wallet-size card with the picture of a saint in prayer. Then his finger was pricked and his blood rubbed onto the picture of the saint. As the picture was set afire, Buscetta pronounced that his flesh would burn like the picture if he should betray the organization.

And betray it he did. Buscetta hadn't yet been burned to a crisp by his former associates, but his family paid a heavy price for his disloyalty. After claiming that more than half of his Sicilian family had already been killed by the Mafia, Buscetta decided to testify about the Sicily-American drug operation before he, too, met his death.

Buscetta's story corroborated what many of us who covered mob trials already knew: The crime families operated on a simple kill or be killed philosophy. We also saw firsthand evidence of that as the trial moved along and important witnesses as well as one or two defendants disappeared; they were later found shot to death gangland-style.

From an artistic standpoint I had the most difficult time sketching one defendant. For whatever reason, Salvatore Castellano kept an eye on me and did his best to hide his face from my view. But I finally obtained the view I needed when he walked right past me in the courthouse cafeteria; he, of course, didn't know that I have almost perfect recall, and I sketched him from memory.

The defense attorneys, however, displayed their vanity time and again, pretending to watch me sketch and then suggesting that I sketch them and their clients. But the most interesting subject of the trial to draw was the Godfather of the Godfathers, Badalamenti. He knew I favored sketching him because every so often he turned his dark eyes from under black, bushy brows and gave me a disapproving stare. His rugged, angular face could have stopped a clock. He didn't miss one piece of testimony, but he appeared to be seething with anger. If he had a gun in court, Badalamenti would have shot at someone or something.

As authorities documented the activities of the drug network, including laundering money from pizza parlors through a Swiss bank before it was sent to Sicily, perhaps Badalamenti understood his destiny. After months and months of testimony, the jury found the twenty-two defendants guilty, and Badalamenti received a forty-year jail sentence.

Yet another important trial began in November 1985, a month after the start of the Pizza Connection proceedings, when the government charged in federal court that Carmine ("The Snake") Persico and ten codefendants of the Columbo family with racketeering and a wide range of other charges. Prosecutors claimed that the crime family existed for the sole purpose of making money in any illegal way, including loan-sharking, gambling, hijacking, extortion, pornography, untaxed cigarette smuggling, counterfeiting, bankruptcy fraud, and union racketeering.

However, prosecutors also pointed out that the family actually shied away from drugs and prostitution and instead had developed many "legitimate" businesses such as funeral homes, real-estate agencies, wine and liquor distributorships, restaurants, and vending machine services in Brooklyn and Staten Island.

The strength of organized-crime struck home when the federal attorneys also noted that a yard of concrete probably hadn't been poured in New York City without a payoff to the Columbo family.

Despite the seriousness of the charges, this trial became somewhat of a theatrical sideshow. It was, of course, immediately noted in court that actor James Caan, who played a major role in *The Godfather,* regularly visited the courtroom. When it was also learned that one of the defendants had been his boyhood friend, the prosecution subpoenaed him.

We also heard taped conversations of Persico offering Internal Revenue Service undercover agent Richard Annicharico a bribe of a quarter-million dollars to obtain an early release for Persico from prison on other charges.

Ralph Scopo, a former concrete workers' union president and codefendant, later interrupted the trial when he complained of chest pains and was taken to a hospital for emergency treatment. Incidentally, Scopo later tried to solicit sympathy during the Mob Commission trial with a story about his wife being ill with cancer.

But Scopo took a beating during the testimony of building contractor Anthony Rivera, who stated under immunity from prosecution that he paid Scopo fifteen thousand dollars after the union president threatened to send him down to Little Italy to make the acquaintance of three or four guys with thick necks and bad dispositions.

Gennaro ("Jerry Lang") Langella provided another comic routine by sniffing, coughing, and generally looking miserable with a bad cold during the same trial. Although he tried to get as much mileage as he could out of not feeling well, the poor man *really* had a terrible infection and looked like Rudolph the Red-Nosed Reindeer. His appearance topped off a fascinating trial that wove together the history of the Columbo crime family and the extent of its empire with such an interesting array of witnesses and defendants.

On the other hand, the 1982 trial of the Bonanno family was no laughing matter and involved FBI undercover agent Donnie Brasco. In fact, Brasco's infiltration of the hierarchy of several crime families—which first became public in this trial—set the stage for the Mob Commission and Pizza Connection trials as well as lesser proceedings against other mobsters. I presumed that plainclothes FBI agents were scattered throughout the courthouse to make sure no one slipped through security checkpoints in the building. Because of the extensive knowledge Brasco had gained about the Mafia, the crime organization reportedly placed a big-money contract to end Brasco's life on the orders of top mob bosses.

Each time Brasco approached the witness stand to testify, a sudden hush swept the courtroom and all eyes focused on the undercover agent. Brasco said that he prepared himself for the assignment by attending FBI seminars on the mob and then participating in a real hijacking with criminals. Setting himself up as a jewel thief, a burglar, and a "fence" for stolen goods, he caught the attention of mobsters and began meeting them in various clubs around New York City. His first real break in the FBI sting came when Brasco started to work as a bookmaker for Benjamin ("Lefty") Ruggerio. Brasco became so successful that other mobsters showed interest in hiring him, and eventually he became a trusted member and handyman for the Bonanno family.

At times Brasco, whose real name is Joseph Pistone, had me mesmerized, and I dropped my pencil on the sketchpad and concentrated on his testimony. His description of mob chieftain Angelo Bruno, who ruled gangland activities in Philadelphia as well as Atlantic City, was particularly insightful. Bruno, whom Brasco said was excessively greedy, refused to allow others a piece of the lucrative Atlantic City rackets. Bruno also created animosity among other mob leaders because he didn't deal drugs in his territory and subsequently lost considerable revenue.

Trying to move Bruno out of his own territory but still hoping to keep him happy, the mob had offered Bruno profits from its activities in Florida. But Bruno stood his ground. His greed and stubbornness, however, earned him a bullet in the head, and a mob war broke out in Philadelphia over who controlled crime activities there.

How Brasco kept his cool—and his life—-throughout

six years of that kind of living is beyond me. He certainly had the physical characteristics for the part of an undercover agent in the mob—Roman-looking with a strong jaw, square face, and high cheekbones, dark but receding hair, and large brown but questioning eyes—as well as the mental toughness to associate with mobsters and to see their criminal activities daily.

Although Brasco claimed in court that he "never encouraged anyone to commit a crime" while working undercover, he had urged "Lefty" Ruggerio to kill mob rival Anthony Mirra. Ruggerio didn't take action, but within a year Mirra's bullet-ridden body was found slumped over the wheel of his car in New York City.

Brasco played the role of a mobster so well that Ruggerio even told him that "Rusty" Rastelli would head the Bonanno family after Carmen Galente's assassination. The FBI mole also witnessed other inner family workings and power struggles, including the death of three captains.

Frankly, I wouldn't have done business with the likes of Brasco. A man who knew how to take care of himself, Brasco also found his undercover assignment "a game of wits" and mob work "boring, lonely, but dangerous."

But Brasco's bravery resulted in prison terms for top mobsters: "Lefty" Ruggerio and Nicholas Santora, fifteen years for racketeering and conspiracy to murder three former *capi;* Anthony ("Mr. Fish") Rabito, thirteen years for drug violations; Vincent Lopez, six years for robbery; and Antonio ("Boots") Tomasulo, five years for racketeering and drug and gambling violations.

Judge Robert Sweet accused the mob of "waging war against society" but said Brasco showed "steadfast courage that was so commendable society owes him a lot."

Frank ("Funzi") Tieri played a different game and paid a higher price during his 1980 trial, in which he was the first man charged with being the head of a crime family. The highlight of the trial was the dramatic and sometimes comical testimony of James ("Jimmy the Weasel")

Fratianno, a former mob hit man turned informer under immunity from prosecution.

Fratianno described La Costra Nostra, a pseudonym for the Mafia, as a secret organization divided into families that conducted criminal activities in twenty major United States cities. Each family controlled one city, with the exception of New York City. Five families, headed by Frank Tieri, Carlo Gambino, Paul Castellano, Anthony Corallo, and Thomas DiBella, ruled rackets in the Big Apple.

Tieri, who at seventy-six wore a patch over his left eye and looked weak and frail, quietly listened to all Fratianno's damning testimony, but his head always jumped up when Jimmy admitted to being a paid government informer. He glared at Fratianno with his one good eye.

Once, however, Tieri caught everyone's attention as he gripped his head, groaned, and collapsed. He was taken out of court and hospitalized. Jay Goldberg, Tieri's attorney, later appealed to the judge to end the trial because his client suffered from diabetes and heart disease. "He's too sick to stand trial," Goldberg said. The judge adjourned rather than dismissed the proceeding.

Never trusting a mob boss who claims illness, the FBI followed Tieri after his hospital release and videotaped him leaving home and traveling around the city. The judge reconvened the trial, Fratianno continued his testimony, and the jury eventually found Tieri guilty of heading the Genovese crime family. Tieri died of natural causes before his sentencing.

The 1979 trial of Anthony M. Scotto, the forty-five-year-old general organizer of the International Longshoremen's Association and president of Local 1814, turned New York City crime kingpins and state politicians on their ears. Scotto, a close ally of New York Governor Hugh Carey, also had been a supporter of former New York City Mayor John V. Lindsay and campaigned for Jimmy Carter during the 1976 presidential election.

From the announcement of the seventy-count indictment, Scotto took a pounding because his codefendant was none other than Anthony Anastasio, executive vice president of Local 1814. The union chapter had been founded by "Tough Tony" Anastasio, the legendary and undisputed czar of the Brooklyn waterfront. To complicate his public-relations and legal problems further, Scotto's personal and family history also became an issue. Scotto, a Brooklyn College dropout, had married the former Marion Anastasia, daughter of crime boss and Murder, Inc., high executioner Albert Anastasia.

The indictment charged Scotto with conspiracy, racketeering, tax evasion, and receiving more than three hundred thousand dollars in payments from waterfront companies, which was illegal under the labor provisions of the Taft-Hartley Act.

Scotto came over to me frequently during recesses, and we discussed art and a wide variety of other topics. I, like many others, was taken by Scotto's charm, and as the trial moved along I became quite sympathetic to his family. It was extraordinarily difficult for them to cope with the daily proceedings because prosecutors hung out all the Scotto personal and family laundry for the jury. No matter what your background, having private family and financial affairs tossed around in the headlines adds to the stress of a criminal proceeding.

From the beginning of his involvement with the union in 1963, Scotto testified that he sought to change the image of waterfront workers from dock ruffians to hardworking men who genuinely cared about their families, city, and country. Using the clout of his half-million-strong union members, he cultivated local, state, and national political figures, including an unknown congressman from Brooklyn named Hugh Carey. Scotto became a political supporter and threw many rallies for top Democratic candidates of the 1960s and 1970s and enjoyed the company of the city's and state's top elected officials.

Unfortunately, as Scotto's political clout grew, so did rumors and accusations about his mob ties. The U.S. Department of Justice in 1969 labeled Scotto a *capo* in the family headed by Carlo Gambino. Scotto denied the charges, but suspicion of him grew stronger when he later invoked the Fifth Amendment before the State Legislative Crime Commission, which asked him outright if he had ever been a member of the Mafia.

What amazed me throughout the trial is that Scotto's political influence prospered throughout the years when those charges were being made. He conducted rallies and fund-raisers for candidates and appeared to be on a first-name basis with our highest elected officials. You would have thought that some politicians might have backed away from Scotto until the controversy was cleared up, but I guess they thought that his union's support was too important for their election or reelection efforts.

The government claimed in its case against Scotto that waterfront companies made payoffs to him to obtain dock business and to decrease the number of accident claims made by longshoremen, and William ("Sonny") Montella, the general manager of a waterfront carpentry firm, sealed Scotto's fate with testimony that he paid Scotto ninety-four thousand dollars in cash for his services. Montella, under oath, said the money definitely wasn't a political contribution of any sort.

Despite this kind of testimony, former governor Carey appeared as a character witness and described Scotto as trustworthy, intelligent, and an effective and dedicated leader. Former New York City mayors Wagner and Lindsay called Scotto a man of integrity.

Defense attorney James LaRossa made an impassioned speech to the jury that Scotto shouldn't be punished for the prominence he had achieved in labor and politics. Presidents, governors, mayors, and countless other public officials had warmly received and respected the defendant. LaRossa declared that Scotto was a considerate man as well as a good father and that he wasn't a common thief and shouldn't be treated like one.

Because I had become so fond of Scotto and his family, I suffered with them when the jury went into deliberation. Unfortunately, the jury found him guilty, and Scotto received a five-year prison term and a seventy-five-thousand-dollar fine. For those of us who knew the Scottos, this truly was a tough trial to endure.

One of the most flamboyant characters ever to walk into a courtroom to face charges of mob activities was the late Anthony ("Tony Pro") Provenzano. From 1975 to 1979 I covered many, many arraignments and trials involving Provenzano, the onetime head of the thirteen-thousand-member Teamsters' Local 560 in Union City, New Jersey.

Provenzano, who always had a huge but smirky smile and wore bifocals, fancied himself as quite a ladies' man. He eyed every woman—and I mean *every* woman—who walked in court and, at the same time, gave off an incredible air that he was innocent of anything that the prosecution charged.

Tony had the look of a middle-class *bon vivant,* and he vehemently denied that he was a part of the Mafia. In fact, he once provided the court with a moment of comic relief when he described the Mafia, which was referred to as the Black Hand Society during his youth, as a fabrication of the FBI, the CIA, and the news media. Provenzano also informed the court that he lived in Florida because all good Sicilians like warm weather.

But several juries didn't buy Tony's humor or his claim of innocence in a number of trials. In 1978 he was convicted of murdering a union foe who had vanished in Ulster County, New York, some seventeen years earlier, and three racketeering convictions—two in New York in 1978 and one in New Jersey in 1979—ended Provenzano's role in mob activities. He spent the last eight years of his life in federal prison and died of congestive heart failure in 1988 in a hospital near Lompac Federal Penitentiary northwest of Los Angeles.

In both life and death, "Tony Pro," who reportedly had been a *capo* in the Genovese family, has been remembered most for his friendship and later for his dislike of former Teamster president Jimmy Hoffa. Bad blood reportedly developed between the friends when they both served time at a federal prison in Lewisburg, Pennsylvania, and Hoffa refused to use his still considerable influence to win back a pension plan that Provenzano lost when he went to jail.

Tony, who once claimed that he was going to bury Hoffa, became a key figure in the latter's disappearance in 1975. The organized-crime and racketeering section of the Department of Justice believed that three Local 560 members closely associated with Provenzano had abducted Hoffa in a parking lot outside of Detroit. Later the strike force claimed that Hoffa's body was stuffed into a fifty-five-gallon drum, carted to Jersey City, and buried in a trash dump. Believe it or not, the government ordered a bulldozer search of the dump for Hoffa's body.

Other rumors about the whereabouts of Hoffa surfaced, but the one most mentioned was the one about Hoffa's body being ground up and put into a slab of cement. But a 1978 book quoted an FBI memo saying that the kidnappers had put Hoffa into a garbage shredder and cremated the remains in an incinerator.

Throughout all his appearances in court on the Hoffa matter, Provenzano kept his cool and his smile. Once, when I was sketching him, he looked at me and said, "If you give me a kiss, I'll pose for you."

The most memorable aspect of the December 1978 trial involving Elliot Weisman, Gregory J. DePalma, and Richard Fusco, who had formed a corporation to run the bankrupt Westchester Premier Theater, was the dastardly testimony of James Fratianno, the self-proclaimed mob hit man who had worked out a deal guaranteeing him a five-year prison term in return for identifying mob members and detailing their activities.

The corporation had been charged with skimming

money from the theater's operation, intentionally driving it into bankruptcy, and involving itself with illegal mob activities.

As part of the case against the defendants, the government introduced a color photograph taken in a dressing room at the theater. Pictured with the defendants were Fratianno, Frank Sinatra (who had appeared three times at the theater but had not been charged with any wrongdoing), and Mafia bosses Carlo Gambino and Paul Castellano, now both dead.

The photograph was, for quite some time, a controversy during the trial. Some figures had been darkened out, and the picture was not immediately released to the press. The significance of the photograph seemed to be that it offered some evidence that the defendants had known the wrong people. I did a sketch of it that appeared in a New York newspaper, and *Life* magazine later ran the picture.

Fratianno, who testified that he had garroted eleven people at the behest of mob chieftains, described the killings with disassociation, as if he was strolling from one room to another. With equal dispassion, he stated that he had turned state's evidence because mobsters had put out a one-hundred-thousand-dollar contract on him. He cooperated with the prosecution in the Westchester case as part of the government's protected-witness program.

Quick Sketches

While sketching cases involving the mob, I heard countless statements from prosecutors about why organized-crime remained strong. But I thought that one of the best explanations about the mob's control over its members was provided by car thief Phillip ("Philly Glass") Masi. He wanted to quit the business because he was instructed by the Gambino family to change vehicle identification numbers of stolen autos in a warehouse next door to a police station in Brooklyn.

"I told Henry Borelli it was crazy to do this sort of thing next door to a police station," Masi said during testimony about Gambino crime activities. "He said it would be no problem; if law enforcement officials ever come in, just tell them you're working for us. If, God forbid, anything happened, there would be no trouble getting lawyers, and if you have to do any time, your family would be taken care of."

But Masi still objected and told Borelli that he wasn't going to work next to a cop station. "He told me that I had no choice in the matter, that I was too involved in the operation," Masi recalled. "Once you worked for the Mafia, you had a job for life—even if you didn't want it."

DURING JOHN GOTTI'S TRIAL ON RACKETEERING CHARGES, the things I immediately noticed about Wilfred ("Willie Boy") Johnson, a former Gotti confidant who had been identified by a prosecutor as an FBI informer, were the unusual tattoos on his knuckles. With one letter on each knuckle, *l-o-v-e* was written on one hand and *h-a-t-e* on the other. Johnson refused to testify against his former boss, and Gotti was acquitted. But everyone assumed Johnson was a man living on borrowed time.

Several years later I remembered the *h-a-t-e* tattoo on Johnson's hand as a symbol of the mob after three men with automatic weapons opened fire on "Willie Boy." Police found him dead, with fourteen bullet wounds in his body. The message was clear: If you crossed the mob, you paid for it with your life.

* * *

Auguste Joseph Ricord, who was accused in 1972 of smuggling two and a half billion dollars' worth of heroin into the United States, gained notoriety in the movie *The French Connection* but turned out to be much more villainous and much less sophisticated than portrayed by Hollywood. After he was extradited from Paraguay to the United States, I covered his arraignment in the French Connection case and discovered that the man was diabolical.

Ricord, originally from Marseille, France, had been an habitual criminal since the age of fourteen with theft, extortion, assault, and gun possession convictions. He worked for the Gestapo during World War II, fled Europe at the war's end, and became a citizen of Argentina. A French military court had sentenced him to death in absentia for his Nazi collaboration. Unlike the attractive and suave actor who played his role in the movie, Ricord himself was a short, balding man who had muttonchop sideburns and wore tortoiseshell glasses. He looked more Slavic than Gallic.

I was often surprised by the humor that mob defendants and their attorneys showed to the courtroom. The case involving Anthony ("Mr. Fish") Rabito, who was moving along in years and sported white hair, made us laugh because the mobster flaunted his ladies' man reputation. He made a point of showing how cool he was by keeping his shirt open to show off the gold chains he wore around his neck.

Rabito, convicted in the Gambino trial that featured Donnie Brasco, claimed he got into trouble because his codefendants brought women to his East Side place and sometimes "they turned my bedroom into a gym. It got so busy that I had to ask them to bring changes of linen." Rabito's lawyer, Paul Rad, Jr., didn't pass up the chance to tell the court that his client "was as clean as a new sheet and has a big heart."

FOUR

Politicians and Radicals

Television has been a prime medium in the coverage of political crime and of political extremism for quite some time in our country. Although many of us haven't exercised our right to vote in elections as frequently as we should, Americans have monitored on the nightly news politicians of all persuasions and their excesses.

The fight for political clout among the nation's major parties has brought high drama from top elected officials in Washington, D.C.; sad images from the politically disenfranchised in New York City and other metropolitan areas; and outright comedy from all those who wanted the power that came with holding a political office.

To me, it seemed television news devoted so much airtime to politicians and political radicals who found themselves in a courtroom because we not only wanted viewers to know about the proceeding but also hoped they formed an opinion about the people involved and about the political ideals they represented. That sometimes maddening combination of public disclosure about our political leaders has become a hallmark of American democracy known as the public's right to know.

Fortunately, I worked in television news during a period when some of the most important conflicts, crises, and controversies of modern America erupted in the courtroom. Because I started at NBC in 1972, I quickly became accustomed to sketching people and events that meant a great deal to the future of the country.

The one Watergate-related trial I covered was that of former U. S. attorney general John Mitchell and former secretary of commerce Maurice Stans, charged with conspiracy to defraud the federal government and with obstruction of justice, in a 1973 trial held in New York's federal court. The charges stemmed from their work for Richard Nixon's 1972 bid for reelection; Mitchell served as campaign manager and Stans as a fund-raiser.

Prosecutors claimed that Stans accepted a secret and illegal two-hundred-thousand-dollar campaign contribution from shady financier Robert Vesco while Mitchell interceded with a Securities and Exchange Commission investigation of Vesco's takeover of a company called Overseas Services Limited.

The courthouse was mobbed with spectators and with national and foreign press people, who were issued pink-numbered tickets for seats. Tensions ran high in the press corps because seats were so limited; only one representative from each network was allowed in the courtroom. Artists, however, sat in the second row.

My reporter for the network, Bob Hager, and I decided that I should represent NBC, since my sketches would visually describe the variety of prospective jurors and the setting of the trial. That meant that a huge responsibility rested on my shoulders. I represented the entire news operation—WNBC (the local affiliate) and NBC News—which meant that I also worked with a local reporter and two field producers.

Prospective jurors begged off any involvement in the trial for many reasons: poor health, fear for their jobs because of the anticipated length of the trial, and responsibilities at home. Judge Lee P. Gagliardi, who had been appointed by President Nixon, listened patiently to each peremptory challenge by the prosecutor and by the defense attorneys and even excused an elderly woman who had difficulty hearing.

I sketched those picked for jury duty as well as Mitchell conferring with his attorneys and Stans meeting with his advisers. After the first full day of the trial, a federal agent escorted the jury out of the courtroom and made sure it was sequestered. It seemed to me that the jury was truly a cross section of America—male and female, white and black, young and old. On the next Monday morning, Mitchell approached me and started what would be a ten-week ritual. He always smiled and winked at me in a polite but flirtatious manner. "I like your sketches," he said with a twinkle in his eye.

The trial attracted a curious assortment of people from all kinds of social strata. As usual, a few oddballs showed up, too. One man, who appeared every day with small signs on his hat, gave incoherent speeches outside the courtroom. Since this was a trial with huge importance, many of the relatives of those involved in the proceeding also attended the trial. Two familiar figures included the judge's wife and the father of Mitchell's attorney.

Everyone watched and listened in awe at the parade of famous witnesses who appeared in court to testify for or against the defendants, the first cabinet members to be accused formally of criminal acts since the Teapot Dome scandal of the 1920s in the administration of President Warren G. Harding. The supporting cast in this trial turned out to be as varied and intriguing as an artist could ever want. I was quite surprised to see a psychologist I had earlier sketched at a meeting my husband attended on hypnosis; he accompanied Shirley Bailey, Vesco's secretary. Although I never figured out what purpose the psychologist served being in court, I suspected he tried to keep Bailey calm before and after her testimony.

Harry Sears, a former New Jersey state senator who was popularly referred to as "the most honest lawyer in New Jersey," testified that he was the man who brought Vesco, Stans, and Mitchell together via his association with the financier's International Controls Corporation. Sears appeared to be quite indifferent as a witness for the prosecution and seemed more intent on telling the court about his high esteem for John Mitchell.

As the ten-week trial slowly continued, the stature of the witnesses increased. However, I became saddened by their poor showing. Not one official who had served in the administration showed brilliance, strength, or depth of character. John Dean, former counsel to President Nixon, seemed well-groomed but nervous and made a poor witness. Edward Nixon looked like a thin version of his brother, the president, while Donald Nixon was a fat one. They reminded me of Stan Laurel and Oliver Hardy. Donald didn't know what to say when he was asked to describe his profession; he looked around the courtroom, smiled, and babbled something about Marriott Hotels being the best in the world. Each Nixon, however, showed his patriotism by wearing a pin topped with an American flag on his coat lapel.

William Casey, who later became the director of the Central Intelligence Agency in the Reagan administration, seemed like an elderly gentleman who had lost his faculties. He had an equally difficult time hearing and speaking.

G. Bradford Cook, a former general counsel to the Securities and Exchange Commission who became its chairman, made a rather pathetic witness. He admitted that he had perjured himself four times in the case, and he seemed generally incompetent.

But Rose Mary Woods, the president's secretary, created a stir. She arrived in front of the courthouse in a limousine and commanded everyone's attention. Everyone knew she *really* knew a great deal about what went on in the Oval Office and about the Watergate mess. Woods, an elderly woman who had deep circles under her eyes accented by long, fake lashes, carried an attaché case that contained a secret White House campaign donor list that became irreverently known as "Rose Mary's baby."

John Mitchell pushed his body forward, listened intently, and clutched reading glasses in his left hand as Woods spoke. Stans, however, looked down at reading material. The government attorneys were excited, and the defense lawyers were anxious as Woods began her testimony about contributors.

The existence of such a list had been revealed in a suit filed by the citizen lobby group Common Cause against the Finance Committee to Reelect the President, but the list had not been publicly available until Woods pulled it out of her attaché case in court.

Woods said the largest contribution had been made by the Amerada Hess Corporation, an oil company that kicked in two hundred fifty thousand dollars to reelect President Nixon. At the time of the contribution, the company faced a Department of the Interior investigation of its oil refinery operations in the Virgin Islands. Several weeks later, the Department of the Interior closed out its investigation of the company without taking any action.

Woods also revealed that William E. Simon, then the director of the federal energy office, had arranged for a one-hundred-thousand-dollar contribution on behalf of his former employer, the investment house Salomon Brothers.

The president's secretary, who wore a pastel suit with ruffles at the neck and at the wrist, was such a contrast to the other witnesses—mostly men—in appearance and in demeanor. She was overly charming and took special care to enunciate properly all the names she read from the list. When she finished her testimony, Rose Mary smiled, looked directly at John Mitchell, and left the courtroom.

W. Clement Stone, the Chicago insurance magnate who contributed two million dollars to Nixon's reelection campaign, dressed rather foolishly for New York's snowy weather by wearing a blue suede coat and blue bow tie covered with white polka dots. The man certainly had money to toss around, but he also struck me as one of the more eccentric corporate leaders in the country.

When Maurice Stans testified on his own behalf, he told a story about going from "outhouse to the White House." Theo Wilson, a reporter for the Tribune Company, and I called him "Mr. Mod" because we thought he wore Pierre Cardin suits. Sketching him was a delight because he became so animated while describing his humble beginnings, his election to the Accountants' Hall of Fame (although he had never received a C.P.A. degree), and his wife's illness and its impact on him. I enjoyed many conversations with Walter Bonner, his defense attorney, and supplied him with Bufferin and hard candy when the courtroom became hot and dry.

One afternoon a comical incident happened to me as I waited outside the courtroom door after the lunch recess. A middle-aged man approached me and asked if I knew where Mitchell could be reached. When I responded with a question about who sent him to find the former attorney general, the man snapped, "Mr. Jimmy Hoffa is serving him with a subpoena." I told him to wait until the federal marshals arrived, and then they would take care of him. If he was legitimate, I'm sure Mitchell was served, and if he was some crackpot, I'm equally sure the man left the building.

Whenever Mitchell himself entered the courtroom, he often teased me with that wink and that ever-present twinkle in his eye. In fact, my friend Theo Wilson dubbed him "Mr. Twinkles." Although I'd never seen him drunk, I also suspected some of his friendliness may have resulted from a bit of tippling in the back room. There were times, however, that he looked red-nosed and appeared to sway.

Mitchell remained aloof in court and only occasionally took notes. He left most of his defense to attorney Peter Fleming, a tall man who carried himself with the disheveled elegance of former New York mayor John Lindsay. As a witness, Mitchell displayed remarkable control as he described his rise in legal circles, his job as attorney general, and his fall from grace. He appeared levelheaded even under cross-examination.

The pressroom, in the basement of the building, was more hectic than normal during this case. I used the top of a newspaper's file cabinet to clean up my drawings and got to know the brilliant Theo Wilson. She worked through lunch as I did, and sometimes we shared a peanut butter sandwich or cheese crackers.

Although we all covered the same story and competed with each other, the press became a close family. Each network, television and radio station, newspaper, wire service, or magazine set up private—and locked—phones, but each day a number of the phones conked out. So we used the working phones of other news organizations and vice versa to meet our deadlines. Perhaps we got along so well because all of us fought exactly the same kinds of pressures and problems daily while covering the trial.

When the judge instructed the jury about its deliberations, reporter Robert Hager read me the riot act about staying close to the courthouse and not going home to New Jersey. If I didn't stay in New York City, he said I'd never again work for NBC. So I called my husband and told him I would be staying in the city until the jury delivered a verdict, and then I called the network's northeastern assignment desk and said I didn't have any makeup, bedclothes, or money. No problem, an editor said. A reservation at the elegant Barclay Hotel would be made, and a courier would deliver expense money to me.

That night turned out to be a huge laugh on me as well as the hotel. After dining out with some media friends at an Italian restaurant and waiting at the courthouse until ten o'clock, I arrived at the hotel carrying my black portfolio.

The dignified gentleman at the reception desk looked at me rather indifferently. I knew I had chalk all over my face, and my stocking had a run in it. Because the soap in the ladies' room at the courthouse had all but disappeared, my hands looked like those of a chimney sweep. I assumed he thought I earned my living another way when he asked, "Yes, madam?" I told him NBC had made a reservation for me, but he firmly asked if I could pay for the room in advance. Instead of telling him I was a good risk, I pulled the rental charge from an envelope filled with crisp twenties.

A snooty bellhop carried my portfolio at arm's length from his clean uniform, and I thought they both believed I was some sort of unsavory character who luckily had enough money to stay in their expensive hotel.

Another day and night came and went before I called my husband to join me in New York City. After three years of forced separation during his military service in World War II, we had rarely slept apart. It was good to feel the warmth and security of his arms at night while I waited for the verdict.

On Sunday morning, Bob Hager told me there wasn't any need to get to court before ten in the morning. Eager beaver that I was, I arrived at my usual nine-thirty, and as I sat down to sketch the room, the court clerk announced that the judge was about to open court. That meant the jury was about to announce its finding. Then panic struck. Bob Hager was, ironically, nowhere to be found. Bob Toombs, our producer, planned to call the assignment for another reporter if Hager didn't show up. Luckily, he did.

When the foreman read the not guilty verdict, all hell broke loose in the courtroom. The press moved en masse to congratulate and to question Mitchell and Stans, who were busy embracing their jubilant attorneys. The victors asked me to join them at an acquittal party at Essex House, and this time I said I would attend. It was such a long, difficult, and important trial. I wanted to be part of it.

Before going to the party, I went back to the station and called my husband, who helped me pick up the close to five hundred sketches I drew during the trial. I went up to the hotel suite by myself, since Ed couldn't find a parking space, and an overjoyed John Mitchell greeted me with a kiss. But I told him my husband was in the car waiting for me, and I couldn't stay long. True to his good-natured courtroom flirtation, Mitchell winced and said, "Ida, don't tell me that you're married?" Then he graciously told me to have the doorman watch the car and bring Ed to the reception.

When I introduced them, Ed said, "If you need a good psychiatrist, I'd be glad to help." Mitchell comically shot back, "When I have the need for a psychiatrist, I'll plead guilty first."

MY FIRST EXPOSURE TO POLITICAL AND RACIAL MILITANTS hit me hard and shattered my naïveté about what happened in someone else's neighborhood. In 1972 I covered the retrial of the so-called Harlem Four. William Prague, Wallace Baker, Ronald Felder, and Walter Thomas had been convicted and each had served eight years in jail for the 1964 murder of Margate Sugar, a Hungarian refugee. She had died during the robbery of the small secondhand clothing store she operated in Harlem, and her husband, Frank, had been stabbed seven times.

What I saw in court was a real eye-opener. The witnesses in the case had been caught in a great number of contradictions. Three defense attorneys, including William Kunstler, also pointed out that a key prosecution witness had recanted his testimony. There didn't seem much of a case left against these men, but juries were never predictable. So instead of taking a chance, the defendants pleaded guilty to a charge of manslaughter. When they did, the prosecutor said he was satisfied that the pleas were voluntary and that the defendants were guilty.

Standing proud and defiant, the defendants listened to the judge's decision to release them in consideration for the time they had already spent in jail. But Kunstler didn't let what he thought a miscarriage of justice slip past him without condemnation. "It is the mark of a truly sick society," he said, "when four young, black men find it necessary to plead guilty for crime they did not commit. It is a tragic reminder that justice is really blind."

Another man was later convicted for the actual murder and was sentenced to life in prison for second-degree murder.

Throughout my career, though, I covered many black and white radicals who at first believed in a cause, became fanatic, and then tried to step over the people they killed in the name of the cause.

The first of four separate trials involving JoAnne Chesimard, a member of the militant Black Liberation Army, took place in December 1973. She, along with fellow militant Fred Hilton, had been charged with taking three thousand seven hundred dollars from a branch of Manufacturers Hanover Trust Company in the Bronx in 1972. Two key government witnesses, who admitted their role in the holdup, testified against Chesimard and Hilton. In turn, Chesimard and Hilton refused to participate in the proceeding, including cross-examination. But the jury apparently didn't like the prosecution's case, which was built on testimony from witnesses with immunity from the crime, and found both Chesimard and Hilton not guilty.

I had never seen a case quite like this one; the forelady got up without the defendants in court and read the verdict that acquitted them of three counts in the indictment—conspiracy, robbery, and assault with a deadly weapon. That usually was the most dramatic moment in a trial, and the defendants generally showed great emotion about the successful end of the proceeding. But nothing happened that time.

However, I later covered Chesimard in Morristown, New Jersey, on a charge of being an accomplice to the murder of a state trooper on the New Jersey Turnpike. The trial had to be moved from Morristown because the judge was unable to find enough people to serve on the jury. Most people, it seemed, had heard about Chesimard's affiliation with militants and had already formed an opinion about the woman or about the case.

William Kunstler represented her, but this time the jury found Chesimard guilty. She was sentenced in March 1977 but escaped in November 1979 and hasn't been seen by authorities since. I caught wind of some rumors from militants that she had found asylum in Cuba, but I found that farfetched, especially since a shopping trip to a New York City specialty market. My husband and I went there one afternoon and noticed a large station wagon parked on the street in front of a barricade. Then I spotted JoAnne Chesimard walking out of the store. She got into the station wagon, the blacks sweeping the street near the car removed the barricade, and they jumped in the car and took off with Chesimard. I'm certain the woman I saw was Chesimard. After all, I sketched her during four separate trials and knew her, especially her face.

The 1973 trial of H. Rap Brown, the leader of the Student Nonviolent Coordinating Committee, took place in the New York Criminal Court Building and brought an interesting assortment of people into the courtroom. Most were black and wore long, white robes with white head coverings set off by a black rope. For a moment they visually transported me to a scene in North Africa, but the faces were different. They weren't Semitic but rather American blacks in costume, and I assumed these people considered themselves Black Muslims.

Security for this trial was tight. Outside the courtroom, barricades kept spectators at bay. When I heard a court guard announce that the press could enter the courtroom, I flashed my press card, which unfortunately didn't have my picture on it. Consequently, a buxom blond female guard came forward and gave me a "going over" with her hands. This exercise was an indignity I had to tolerate if I wanted to gain entrance to the courtroom.

Fortunately, I found a front-row seat with an excellent view of the defendant. Brown, who wore a beige knit skullcap and Fidel Castro-like khaki shirt, looked pale and wan—almost ascetic. He certainly didn't fit the picture I had in my mind of the militant who preached that "violence . . . is as American as cherry pie." Next to him sat William Kunstler, the tireless defender of so many militants. The attorney wore a green coat, and his skin somehow reflected a greenish hue. To my surprise, he greeted me like a long-lost friend. But it was the first time I met the man, and I figured he must have worked with my twin sister, Freda, then an illustrator for ABC, at another trial.

We all stood when the judge entered, and then the most unusual thing happened. With a quiet courtroom, Brown took the place of Kunstler to deliver an opening statement. Brown turned his palms to the heavens, murmured something, and then addressed the jury. He spoke of philosophy, religion, and law, then squarely looked at the jury and questioned whether they were his peers (two of the twelve were black). "Man-made law," Brown said, "is not the ultimate law."

Jack Litman, the assistant district attorney handling the case, charged that Brown and three other defendants had entered the Red Carpet Lounge on Manhattan's Upper West Side early on an October morning in 1971 and forced customers to lie face down on the floor, relieved them of their money and their jewelry, emptied the cash register, and sprayed the place with bullets as they left. Two policemen were wounded, and Brown was shot and then captured by police on a nearby rooftop.

A colorful procession of characters testified for the prosecution, including the owner of the lounge. When asked to identify the man who had held a gun to him and inflicted injury, the bar owner, who was a very tall black man, stood up in the elevated witness box and pointed at Brown. The bar owner's height combined with the dramatic gesture made the man a forceful and believable witness. He had an overwhelming presence on the witness stand.

Like so many other areas set aside for the media to prepare their stories, the pressroom in that courthouse was unattractive and filled with old chairs and worn tables. The walls, however, offered a special attraction: media graffiti. A yellow, 1930s-vintage poster offered a reward for information about the disappearance of Judge Crater. Autographed photos hung everywhere, but I especially noticed one of a reporter named Bob who shook hands with Robert Wagner. Underneath it someone had printed, "All Bob's Piss."

Once, when I was cleaning up a good sketch of Brown, I saw a tall black man standing over me. Knowing that Black Muslims had earlier warned me not to sketch them, I thought for sure that the man would grab the piece and shred it.

Instead, he stared at the sketch, and I sneaked a peak at a paperback edition of a book about revolution that he carried in one hand. Suddenly the man's face broke into a huge smile. "That's a great sketch of Rap," he said. "I should know; I'm his brother." With a sigh of relief, I continued to put my work in order for the camera crew and for the reporter.

Since I was new to television news, I enjoyed watching Jimmy Breslin at work. In addition to his newspaper column, he expressed his views in television commentaries and sometimes popped into the Brown trial. Breslin was a bear of a man who seemed to know everyone—the courthouse guards, the prosecutors, the defendants, the reporters.

The least expected reaction that I received from anyone at the Brown trial was from Mrs. H. Rap Brown. A real beauty with café au lait skin coloring and a small, doll-like face, she sat quietly each day and listened to the testimony. Her exotic African headdresses, made with multicolored cottons, always caught my eye.

She confided in me that she wished the network would make a composite of all my sketches for her. That surprised me because I didn't think that those who swore off white establishment practices would succumb to vanity. On the other hand, no one in the courtroom seemed surprised when the jury returned a guilty verdict against Brown.

I inadvertently met another radical in 1976 in the Kabul, Afghanistan, airport while on a medical tour with my husband, a physician. But this one turned out to be quite different and much more dangerous than any radical I had ever met in the United States.

The Ayatollah Khomeini stood out in the crowd at the airport, and my eyes immediately focused on him. He was the center of attention, as if he were a bright light. He was of medium height, and he wore a magnificent and elegant white turban trimmed in gold and a pale blue caftan, also trimmed in gold. He carried a large, blue-velvet-covered book that I assumed was the Koran.

Amid the drab and shabby-looking airport filled with such sad and tattered people, Khomeini loomed larger than life. His dignified beard and mustache and dark, beady eyes, which riveted into space as if he were some kind of holy man, mesmerized me. I got out my sketchbook and materials and immediately began drawing this extraordinary man. All the while, my local guide watched me and suddenly broke my concentration. "That's a beautiful drawing. Do show it to him," the guide urged. "He's a well-known religious leader living in exile from Iran."

I hesitated because I knew that Moslems didn't like to

be photographed or drawn. In the end, though, I approached him, and he smiled when I showed him the sketch. "Is this for me?" he asked in broken English. Instead of giving him the sketch outright, I asked for his card and said I would sent it to him later. Then he wanted to know if I was an American and didn't seem the least bit disturbed or upset when I told him I was a U.S. citizen.

Actually, he was very elegant and very charming, and we continued our conversation in French. When he gave me his card, which provided a Paris address, he said he would love to have the sketch I had completed. Then, of all things, he agreed to pose with me while my husband took our picture. He seemed such a kindly man, such a soft-spoken man. It was very hard to equate him with the tyrant who later emerged.

After he gained power in Iran and after the abduction of our citizens from the embassy in Tehran, I decided to write Khomeini a letter to remind him of our meeting in Afghanistan and to ask for the release of the hostages. And I included the picture of us taken at the airport. "I have hesitated sending this photo for some time," I wrote. ". . . Fate plays strange tricks, and I could not believe that the most charming gentleman I'd met with the sad eyes—who was away from country and family—could be you. When you asked me where I was from, you seemed so cordial when I said the United States of America. What made you change? If anyone would know the anguish of being separated from family and loved ones, it would be you, the man I met who seemed so full of compassion.

"I have heard that you are ill, and I do wish you a speedy recovery. But please, please release the American hostages. The treatment of visitors to Islamic countries has been legendary; one was always treated so graciously. . . . Let every mother's son return. Let there be peace."

I also mentioned that I would send the original sketch if our hostages were returned. Khomeini sadly kept both my picture and our hostages, but that wasn't my last involvement with the Iranian situation. Shortly after I sent Khomeini the letter, NBC News called with an assignment to cover U.S. Attorney General Benjamin Civiletti's appearance before the World Court at The Hague, Netherlands, to urge the release of the hostages.

It was an important assignment. I immediately agreed, packed my art materials, and took a plane to Europe. The setting for the hearing was truly an artist's dream—a magnificent room done with beautiful woodwork containing intricate carvings and huge chandeliers that sparkled like jewels. I thought that the courtroom was even more breathtaking than what I had seen at Versailles, outside of Paris.

A spacious banquet table accommodated the judges while delegates from U.N. countries sat at smaller tables; the international press found themselves at one large table. Directly in front of me stood an empty table reserved for Iran, which failed to send a representative to argue its case. Perhaps that old adage—possession is nine tenths of the law—applied to Iran. Since they held our hostages, the Iranians undoubtedly felt that they didn't have to plead their case in any court of law.

I carefully listened to Civiletti make his argument for the release of our hostages, but the judges didn't seem terribly impressed. His presentation fell on deaf ears, and nothing was resolved. I completed a number of sketches in that wonderful courtroom but was struck by the great contradiction of the proceeding. Despite the artistic magnificence of the room and the seriousness of the proceeding, the tribunal, like the United States, couldn't do anything to force the release of our hostages.

On the domestic front, underground radicals began to surface voluntarily in 1977 in the United States with the reappearance of Mark Rudd, one of the infamous and most inflammatory of the college dissidents. As president of the Columbia University chapter of Students for a Democratic Society, he led protests that paralyzed the campus in 1968 and then played a major role in the four violent "days of rage" in Chicago in 1969.

Rudd had been slapped with a relatively minor charge—criminal trespass—but jumped his bond of two thousand five hundred dollars and disappeared. He had reportedly joined the underground and the more violent Weathermen group, and the FBI conducted a nationwide search for him and placed Rudd on its Most Wanted list.

When Rudd reappeared in New York's Criminal Court, I was absolutely surprised to see a clean-cut young man who wore short hair; horn-rimmed glasses; and a tan, suede jacket instead of a long-haired and unkempt yippie.

Judge Milton Williams, a black man, presided at the hearing. When he asked about Rudd's whereabouts for the previous eight years, attorney Gerald Lefcourt snapped, "He hasn't made any statement to the district attorney's office, and he doesn't intend to do so here."

Rudd, through his attorney, apparently had made some sort of agreement with the prosecutor for his immediate release without bail after he voluntarily surrendered, and the judge wasn't in the least bit pleased. However, Rudd broke his silence and turned political critic with a comment about bail. "It's still W.S.P.," Rudd cracked. "Eight years have gone by, and it still stands for 'White Skin Protection.' "

But before he released Rudd on his own recognizance, Judge Williams sniped back at Rudd. "My concern," he said passionately, "is that be he rich or poor, black or white, a small person or a large person, no bail-jumper should likely be allowed to walk out of the court on his own promise that he would come back when called."

Beginning in 1980, quite a few former student activists and radicals jumped back into the mainstream of life and accepted responsibility for the criminal charges against them. Cathlyn Wilkerson, a petite white woman with blond bangs, pleaded guilty to felony weapons charges resulting from a Greenwich Village dynamite blast that killed three of her political comrades in 1970.

Judge Harold Rothwax, a no-nonsense man who didn't tolerate insincerity, asked the thirty-five-year-old activist where she had been since March 6, 1970, the day she ran nude from the rubble of her family's West Eleventh Street town house, which served as headquarters and bomb factory for the underground political group. Wilkerson, however, made it perfectly clear that the political and social fervor that led her down the path of violence and the creation of a bomb factory was still very much alive inside her.

But Wilkerson also claimed that she wanted to take responsibility for her actions so she could put them behind her and begin a new life working aboveground against the social conditions that originally drove her to radical political action. Finally, she said she'd continue to oppose the practice and principle of imperialism. At that point, I lost my own patience with the woman.

She later seemed slightly defiant but looked the judge straight in the eye with a closing statement: "I have made this decision to plead guilty for a number of reasons," she said.

"In the first place, I do not want to discuss my own deep regrets over the death of three beloved comrades at a sensational trial. I dislike the prospect of the daily publicity that goes with this type of trial, and thirdly, my father has already been threatened with a grand jury subpoena. I don't want to expose members of my family, my friends, and my associates to such personal and political harassment. I want to start new. I'm anxious to start a new life and put the difficulties of the past behind."

What a pathetic situation. I applauded Wilkerson for coming forward and taking the punishment she deserved for her crime, but I didn't understand why on earth she waited so long to acknowledge some of the moral responsibility that all of us must bear when it comes to family and society.

Just after Wilkerson pleaded guilty to reduced charges, the clown prince of the Yippies, Abbie Hoffman, surfaced, and I was off again to cover more courtroom theatrics. Somehow Hoffman and attorney Gerald Lefcourt bypassed Judge Rothwax, who had originally slashed the ex-Yippie leader's 1974 bail in half on charges of selling thirty-eight thousand dollars' worth of cocaine to an undercover agent. After making bail, Hoffman disappeared and lived underground until he gave himself up in September 1980 to a special narcotics officer.

Instead of Rothwax, Hoffman and Lefcourt found themselves in the court of Judge Williams, who had handled the Mark Rudd case. I had a prime seat in the jury box for Hoffman's appearance and probably observed him with greater clarity in court than anyone except the judge. As he entered the courtroom, Hoffman smiled and said, "It's good to be back. I love New York." Then he became very serious. I sensed that Hoffman was a man of many moods and that beneath that big grin was considerable sadness. He looked older than his forty-three years and seemed to have a respectable sloppiness about him. His receding hairline and gray-flecked hair, thick sideburns, and scruffy beard and mustache somehow perfectly matched his red, white, and blue flannel shirt.

By this time, the courtroom seemed to be bursting at the seams with media people and anxious onlookers. Hoffman, who had been the leader of a generation of angry young Americans, still attracted a crowd wherever he went. He knew that, and I thought he was secretly gratified that he still had such a faithful following.

I wondered what made him tick. William Kunstler had once said that Hoffman "taught people how to bring theater into political demonstration. He was able to create political protests by creating laughter."

I caught one final glimpse of Hoffman, who then had

a twinkle in his eye as he flashed the peace sign at the judge. Hoffman moved through the mob of people and answered questions on his way out of the courthouse. In my mind, there was no question about the fact that Hoffman considered his court appearance a show, no matter how serious it was to him in personal consequences. And Abbie Hoffman, clown prince of political protesters, still had the magic to hype a crowd.

Hoffman appeared at his next hearing as scheduled and heard from the judge that a grand jury had returned a new indictment against him on a charge of jumping his ten-thousand-dollar bail in 1974, when he went underground. He was held for one night in jail and then released.

Later, after facing all the charges against him and spending time in prison, I sadly read about Hoffman's suicide in 1989. He was engaged in environmental work and protest in New Hope, Pennsylvania, and was extremely well liked and valued by the people there. No one will ever know what transpired in Hoffman's mind, but his death seemed tragic for a showman who helped mobilize his generation's political views on Vietnam and other issues.

AN EQUALLY SAD EVENT OCCURRED IN 1981 WHEN SENATOR Harrison A. Williams, Jr., a Democrat from New Jersey, became a defendant in one of the three Abscam trials that charge various elected government officials with bribery, conspiracy, and influence-peddling.

Once again, I worked this trial with two reporters and two producers. And, like other trials, I also had a chance to become acquainted with Williams; his wife, Jeanette; and their best friends, who also attended the trial.

The prosecutor said Williams had agreed to use his influence as a senator to win government titanium contracts for a phony Arab sheik, who had been employed by the FBI as a part of its sting of corrupt government officials.

Harrison Williams' case, along with the Abscam trials, had generated a great deal of controversy about the FBI's investigation techniques and about whether the trials were initiated for political purposes by highly placed Washington insiders.

Nonetheless, I watched the proceeding with sadness as Harrison, who had reached the height of power in the Senate, fell into the pits. Over the years he had sponsored valuable labor and social welfare legislation. On the personal front, he had admitted and had beaten alcoholism. After the jury found Williams guilty, Judge George Pratt sentenced him to three years in prison. "In my heart," Williams later told the press, "I know I did no wrong. That makes the verdict most difficult to bear."

Harrison Williams thus became the first sitting senator in seventy-six years—and only the third in U.S. history—to be convicted of a criminal charge. But his agony and public embarrassment hadn't yet ended. The Senate was to take up its ethics committee report on Williams and begin debate on an expulsion resolution.

I covered the proceedings in the Senate chamber. When the debate began, many pleas on behalf of Williams were ignored by senators who wanted him out. Even Senator Bill Bradley, who reportedly viewed Williams as both friend and mentor, said unkind things about Williams in a speech. Rather than face an expulsion vote, Williams resigned. The last senator to resign under that pressure was a Michigan Republican, Truman H. Newberry, who had been convicted in 1922 of election fraud.

In 1982 I covered a somewhat bizarre trial that involved Henry Kissinger, the former national security adviser and secretary of state, and his wife, Nancy. It was a simple assault case brought by Ellen L. Kaplan, a member of a militant political group called the Fusion Energy Foundation.

Kaplan charged that Nancy Kissinger tried to choke her at Newark International Airport after the Kissingers had returned from Boston, where Henry had undergone heart bypass surgery.

During her testimony, Kaplan demonstrated for the court how Nancy had put her hand around her neck, as if she were going to choke Kaplan. But Nancy contradicted Kaplan's story and stated that all she did was shake the young woman after she accosted the couple, screamed obscenities, and charged that Henry Kissinger had slept in a motel with little boys. Unassuming and sincere in her testimony, I thought the court believed Nancy.

When Henry testified, he became very animated. With his thick German accent, he precisely recalled the airport encounter. He said that when Kaplan appeared in front of them and started screaming, Nancy was so angry at what the woman said that she wanted to tell her to stop the verbal tirade. But during the exchange, Nancy put her hand on Kaplan's shoulder. Kissinger claimed that the woman obviously wanted to create an incident out of the meeting, and that was why she brought the matter into court.

I sketched like mad to capture Henry and Nancy because they were so well-known and because I had heard so much about Henry's exploits while serving Presidents Nixon and Ford. He indeed was a joy to sketch and to watch in court. He even sat down next to me, and in his great deadpan manner, said, "You know, I think you gave me too many chins." His comment caught me off guard, and I roared with laughter as I thought that I hoped the man didn't consider himself slender.

Judge Julio Fuentes, who had a reputation for his straightforward manner, ruled that Nancy displayed a somewhat human reaction to the offensive remarks made by Kaplan when the scuffle erupted, and he found Nancy not guilty. And despite the fact that I gave him an extra chin or two, Henry autographed the sketch before he left the courtroom.

Facing a judge and a jury has been a humbling experience for most of the people I've seen in court. If a person also happened to be well known or otherwise in the news, courtroom appearances carried even more weight and undoubtedly more impact on one's friends and family.

That was the case in 1984 and 1985 when I covered a series of hearings involving John Zaccaro, the husband of former Democratic vice presidential candidate Geraldine Ferraro. He faced a fraud charge stemming from a failed real-estate deal.

A proud-looking man, he held his head high and didn't answer any questions from a horde of reporters who surrounded him entering and leaving the courthouse. However, I gained the choicest seat in court when the judge nodded me access to the jury box to complete my sketches.

At one point Zaccaro said, "I just hope this doesn't get nasty." Well, it did. Rumors ran rampant against Zaccaro, and then television and newspaper stories picked apart his personal life, including financial dealings. It truly seemed as if the family couldn't dig themselves out of the media's grip because of the charges against Zaccaro.

When he pleaded guilty in front of Judge George Roberts to charges of scheming to defraud, altering an appraisal report, and overstating his net worth, John Zaccaro did so in a very, very quiet voice. The judge then sentenced him to one hundred fifty hours of community service. Zaccaro left the courtroom in a dignified manner and with the protection of security people.

However, the media ran after him and shouted questions in an undignified manner until he was whisked away from the courthouse. But defense attorney Arthur Liman took on reporters and denied that a plea had been entered as part of a deal that precluded a jail term or more serious charges. The district attorney, a Democrat, stated that Geraldine Ferraro hadn't been aware of the indictments against her husband, and the charges would have been filed even if she hadn't become a candidate.

Liman, however, maintained that Zaccaro would never

have been prosecuted if his wife hadn't run for national office and obtained prominence as the first woman of a major political party to run for vice president. Ferraro, who stood by her husband throughout the entire affair, said in 1985, "He freely admitted to making a mistake, and I'm proud of him for this."

Quick Sketches

The death of New York State Senator Allard Lowenstein, a popular liberal lawmaker, was a case that made me shake my head in disbelief. Lowenstein had been shot in 1980 by Dennis Sweeney, one of his supporters. After Sweeney was charged with the murder, it was discovered that the man actually had ground his teeth down to the gums because he thought that Lowenstein had planted bugs in his teeth.

Poor Sweeney. Not only was he emotionally disturbed, but Sweeney, who was in his thirties, looked at least fifty years old because of the great number of creases and wrinkles in his face caused by the toothless mouth. Judge Stanley Gartenstein, a former rabbi, sent Sweeney to an institution for the criminally insane. There wasn't a soul in the courtroom who didn't feel pity for this very, very sick man.

FORMER SENATOR EDWARD W. BROOKE OF MASSACHUSETTS took a pounding in 1978 in Boston Probate Court when wife, Remigia, whom he married in Italy during World War II, asked for a divorce and accused Brooke of misappropriating funds. Brooke, said Remigia, had made her mother give a gift of forty-nine thousand dollars to family members after her 1965 car accident rendered her an invalid. Remigia claimed that Brooke then put her mother on public welfare and medical assistance.

The senator, who had been defeated in a reelection bid, looked exasperated and lost. There seemed to be such bad blood between husband and wife, and it was sad for me to see love turn to hate after the couple had been married for so many years.

NBC LEGAL REPORTER CARL STERN AND I FLEW TO A FEDeral correctional facility in Pennsylvania in 1977 to cover the release of G. Gordon Liddy after serving time for his role in the Watergate break-in. Prior to his release, Liddy made a brief appearance before a judge, and it seemed as if jail hadn't softened the man or changed his morals. He walked in a defiant manner, with his head held high. When I looked into his eyes, I sensed that he was laughing. But I couldn't figure out if Liddy was laughing at himself or at others.

Although he had been on a hunger strike, Liddy looked fit and appeared to have done considerable exercise in prison. He showed no remorse when the judge questioned him about his role with the Watergate "plumbers." Liddy said that he was proud of what he had done and would do it again if given the chance. I was struck by the fact that Liddy was so sure of himself. I didn't like the way he talked, and I thanked God that Liddy no longer was close to government officials in Washington, where he could instigate a lot of trouble.

FRANK STURGIS, WHO HAD BEEN INVOLVED IN THE WATERgate break-in, found himself in court again in 1977 when he was arraigned in New York Criminal Court for the attempted murder of his girlfriend, Marita Lorenz. She claimed that he threatened her with a gun because she had talked to authorities about circumstances involving Sturgis and the assassination of President Kennedy. The woman claimed that Sturgis, a refugee who had served in the Cuban hills with Fidel Castro and Che Guevara during the Cuban Revolution, and she went to Dallas and met Oswald.

In court I sat next to Sturgis, a self-admitted double agent, and said, "I read that you were in Dallas with Oswald." Sturgis quickly turned to me and said, "Who is Ozzie? I never met the man in my life." I'm still haunted by his reply. If he didn't know Oswald, why did he so quickly blurt out the name Ozzie, as if he *really* knew him?

THE SENTENCING OF CONGRESSMAN FREDERICK W. RICHMOND of New York was a pathetic sight. Judge Jacob Weinstein allowed me to sit in the jury box while he moved off the bench to a table usually used by defendants or the prosecutors and sat opposite Richmond. The defendant, who was gay, had earlier pleaded guilty to possession of marijuana, and during the proceeding it was learned the illegal substance had been obtained for Richmond by his congressional staff.

The affair resulted in Richmond's resignation from Congress, and a few days prior to his sentencing a young man had committed suicide in Richmond's apartment. The whole mess hit Richmond hard. As he sat in front of the judge and learned he would be spending a year in prison, Richmond looked so unhappy and so gaunt that it still haunts me.

THE 1979 QUEENS TRIAL OF PUERTO RICAN SEPARATIST William Morales on charges of criminal possession of firearms and explosives made it painfully clear to the country how far some people were willing to go to achieve their political goals. Morales, a notorious member of the FALN terrorist organization, had been injured while making an explosive device he had hoped to use to blow up an office building in New York City. The premature explosion had caused Morales to lose his right hand, several fingers on the other hand, and his left eye.

Yet during the trial the defendant still was defiant. The judge refused to allow Morales to make political speeches in court, and when his followers shouted their disapproval, he ejected them from the courtroom.

I actually worried about my own safety during the incident but kept my head down and sketched away. Looking at the severe scars on Morales' face made me think that no one had ever told him that life was precious.

In 1980 I covered the Greensboro, North Carolina, trial of four Klu Klux Klansmen and two Nazis who were charged with shooting and killing five people participating in a Communist Party parade. From the moment I heard people shouting ugly political slogans outside the courthouse, I knew that this was going to be a difficult trial.

When the defendants walked into the court, my instincts were proven correct. I was disgusted by what I saw. They looked evil and mean; I had thought that Neanderthal man had disappeared from earth, but no, he still resided in North Carolina. Those men were the meanest and ugliest-looking I had ever seen in my life.

After the judge began the proceeding, a woman whose husband had been killed in the parade screamed, "Long live the Communist Party, and long live the working class." A black woman picked up the chant, and the judge, in a thick southern accent, said, "Put a gag on that woman."

She was indeed gagged by court personnel, and the whole scene appalled me. It all was so repulsive, so ugly. When the all-white jury found the defendants not guilty, I got out of town as fast as I could and went home to New Jersey to breathe some fresh air. The Greensboro that my husband and I had so enjoyed during his posting to an Air Force base there during World War II certainly had fallen into decay and hard times.

* * *

Perhaps one of the most memorable court proceedings I ever covered was the arraignment and trial of Kathy Boudin, who with other members of the Radical Weather Underground, held up a Brinks armored truck with automatic weapons and sawed-off shotguns. In what was described as a "wild West armored-truck robbery," two policemen and a Brinks guard were shot and killed as the radicals made off with one million six hundred thousand dollars in Nyack, New York.

Boudin also had been sought by police after the radical group's New York bomb factory had exploded on West Eleventh Street in Manhattan. The various aspects of the trial covered a two-year period, from 1981 to 1983, but an unforgettable moment occurred when Boudin pleaded guilty to murder and robbery.

She faced the families of the victims and incredibly said, "Nothing can take away the loss. I feel your pain." Then she had the gall to hold her head high and explain her motives. "Although underground for twelve years, a step I took initially because of my opposition to the war in Vietnam and the repression of the Black Movement, I think I remained essentially the same person. I don't like being in jail. No one does. But the meaning of my life has come from being part of a worldwide tradition, a fighting for a more just and humane world. My ideals give me strength today as well as yesterday and tomorrow."

The judge didn't buy any of that rhetoric and sentenced Boudin to a twenty-years-to-life prison term. As long, controversial, and sad as this case was, my own hard work resulted in an Emmy Award nomination for the courtroom portraiture I produced when the jury returned its verdict.

FIVE

Rich, Famous, or Notorious

AMERICA ALWAYS HAS HAD A PARTICULAR FASCINATION WITH celebrities, especially if they are engulfed by controversy or scandal, and I've thought that our preoccupation with public figures constitutes a polite form of emotional voyeurism. Although the press has provoked some bad blood by insisting on its First Amendment rights, we as a society have secretly laughed, cried, and otherwise reveled in the ups and downs of the rich, the famous, and the notorious.

Because I saw celebrities in a not-so-pleasant environment, which often required them to hang out their personal, family, or financial laundry, I also witnessed the best and the worst of our most visible citizens.

Without question, the most dignified personality I sketched in court was Jackie Kennedy Onassis. I first saw Jackie O. in 1972 just after I signed with NBC and was sketching another trial in federal court. Actually, I had been asked by the station to replace the artist who was assigned to the Onassis case because the sketches of that proceeding had been lackluster. However, I declined to do so because I couldn't do that to another artist no matter how important the assignment or how famous the plaintiff might be. In that case, Jackie had objected to paparazzo photographer Ron Galella's tactics in obtaining pictures of her and her family for various publications and went to court to see if she could put an end to his shenanigans. The judge had ordered that the photographer not come within twenty-five feet of Jackie and her family.

Well, in 1983 Jackie was back in court facing the same dilemma with Galella. He had disobeyed the order and reportedly had harassed the family with his zealousness to obtain photographs.

This time I covered the entire proceeding, and Jackie so impressed me as a woman and as a caring mother. Exuding such a subtle manner of grace mixed with shyness, she took notice of everything in the courtroom. She smiled at me, as if acknowledging that I was sketching her, turned away and looked out shyly across the courtroom, and then stared at the material she brought to court as reference material.

While sketching her, I also noticed a certain sadness about her and a certain distrust of other people. She didn't express an outward anxiousness about the hearing, but it was obvious that Jackie wasn't happy about being there, either. I also found her to be a most attractive woman who packaged herself impeccably. Her hair was groomed to perfection in a bouffant style, and her eyes, which seemed to be a bit too far apart on her face, twinkled and showed, at least to me, that she was indeed a sincere person who had a lot of intellectual depth.

Jackie was a joy to sketch. My drawing seemed so effortless because she sat with perfect posture, and I quickly captured her high cheekbones, expressive mouth, and slim but well-proportioned figure. Wearing a lovely dark purple dress that seemed made for her, Jackie personified that old adage about never being too thin or too rich. What did surprise me, though, was Jackie's wispy voice; I thought it similar to that of Marilyn Monroe.

Caroline Kennedy, then unmarried, also testified about the antics of Galella. Unlike her mother's firm manner, Caroline's statements seemed slightly naïve and immature, as if she had been protected from direct questioning most of her life. However, she made it quite plain to the court that Galella had frightened her and had almost made her fall when he sprang out from behind bushes to take her picture as she rode past him on a bicycle.

Many of Jackie's friends also testified about the photographer's often rude and pushy manner while in pursuit of Jackie and the Kennedys. Palimony attorney Marvin Mitchelson, from Los Angeles, represented Galella. In this case the client and the counsel appeared to be a perfect team. Mitchelson, known for his own aggressiveness and flamboyant style in the courtroom, relished his verbal sparring with Jackie. In fact, I wondered if he was being paid for his time or if he took the job as a means to generate publicity for his legal practice.

Jackie held her ground throughout the proceedings and politely responded to all questions. She even placed her vanity aside and put her glasses on to read papers given to her on the witness stand by Mitchelson. But for some unexplainable reason, Judge Irving Cooper interrupted the proceedings three or four times to tell all of us in the courtroom about his early impoverished life. I found those details to be totally irrelevant to the trial, but perhaps it was because of the media throng—he wanted people to know that he was a man with a rags-to-riches story.

After the appearance of all witnesses, the judge ruled that Galella would have to stay twenty-five feet or more away from Jackie and her family or be penalized or fined. I was pleased with the ruling. Despite the fact that I worked in the media, I believed that good taste and honorable ethics are part of any reporter's, photographer's, or illustrator's responsibility in covering the news and personalities. Galella violated those rules, and I'm glad he got his hand slapped for pushing too hard.

Without self-imposed restraint in some areas, the media can make life miserable for and invade a celebrity's right to *some* privacy. The first Jackie court appearance was a perfect example. Because he would have been hounded by reporters, film crews, and gawkers, Aristotle Onassis didn't accompany Jackie during the original hearing against Galella in 1972. Instead Onassis read a newspaper in the park across the street from the courthouse, walked over to his limo when it rolled around the corner to pick him up, and then waited in the safety of the locked car for his wife to leave the building, when he extracted her from the shouting, pushing, and shoving that always accompanied celebrity plaintiffs or defendants.

Looking back at both hearings involving Jackie, I'm glad that she won, and that I had a second opportunity to sketch her in court. I cherished the New York Press Club Award given to me for my portraiture of the former First Lady during her legal bout with a paparazzo nearly as much as my two Emmys. In a way, the award turned out to be a vindication for those of us who worked in television news but often were accused of coldheartedness or brashness. We covered Jackie's courtroom battle but did so in a responsible and professional manner.

ALTHOUGH PLAINTIFFS OR DEFENDANTS KNEW THAT MY illustrations would be used in television coverage of their cases, they frequently viewed me as an artist rather than a journalist, and that opened many avenues of personal contact with them normally denied to reporters and to photographers. My illustrations of former Beatle John Lennon and Yoko Ono eventually led to quite an unexpected and memorable encounter with Yoko after the tragic shooting of her husband.

Our association went back to a controversial and difficult time for the couple in 1974, when it was rumored that the Nixon administration, under the alleged influence of former attorney general John Mitchell, tried to deport Lennon and Yoko because of the "negative impact" they purportedly made on America's youth through the promotion of rock 'n' roll and drugs.

As soon as I was given the assignment to cover a hearing in federal court in the deportation case, I went directly to the courtroom to get the background drawn before the proceedings started. I frequently did this when I thought it might be a quick affair with everyone stating their position and then the court immediately making a ruling in the case.

My reporter, Bob Teague, alerted me the moment John and Yoko walked into the courtroom. The former Beatle was rather thin even in those days and wore his hair long but looked quite natty in a conservative brown suit with an open-collared shirt. Since I had an ideal view of Lennon from the jury box, I completed my sketch in fifteen minutes and then suddenly decided to play autograph-seeker on behalf of my daughter, Lois, an aspiring singer and actress.

After introducing myself, I immediately felt comfortable with the man. He took the sketch and gave it a thorough once-over. "That's a jolly good sketch of me," Lennon said. "Very good, very good indeed." With those words he drew a small caricature of himself and signed the piece, "With love to Lois from John Lennon." Although the judge ruled that Lennon was to appear later in federal court for a formal deportation proceeding, I was beside myself; Lennon had enjoyed my sketch and turned it into a collector's item for my daughter.

The trial generated an extraordinary amount of publicity because of the circumstances leading up to Lennon's court appearances. His immigration status, it was rumored, came under scrutiny by conservative Washington politicians after the singer had been arrested in Great Britain on a minor marijuana charge. In the late 1960s and the early 1970s there seemed to be great debate and true moral conflict in this country about the influence of antiwar protesters, the popularity of groups like the Beatles and the political views they promoted on and off the stage, and the role of so-called recreational drugs in the lives of young adults.

A dozen or so friends and supporters of Lennon attended the trial, and actress Gloria Swanson, despite her frail condition, and Japanese sculptor Isamu Noguchi testified on behalf of the former Beatle. Yoko wore a long, flowing pastel print dress, and that was the first time I saw her pregnant. When the judge ruled that the Lennons would be granted green cards and could remain in the United States, the Lennon supporters decided to throw a party that evening and even invited me. However, I declined because the commute back home to New Jersey would be so late.

The Lennons continued to live in New York City, and I didn't hear too much about them until I received a phone call from Jim Unchester of our assignment desk at three in the morning. When he told me that John had been murdered and the suspected killer, Mark David Chapman, was to be arraigned in Manhattan, I got out of bed, shivering. It was such a shock. All I could think of was the gentle, soft-spoken John Lennon who so admired my sketches. Like most media people who have worked with a celebrity or a newsmaker, images of the person kept repeating themselves in my mind. The tragedy, of course, had become quite personal.

Living approximately fifty miles from the city, I arrived in New York at dawn and waited for Chapman in what seemed like a more depressing than normal criminal court. The judge allowed illustrators to sit close to the accused killer, and I did a good sketch of a fat, bespectacled young man who stared into space and didn't seem to be part of the proceedings. It was a pathetic scene. As we all were to discover, Chapman killed the singer so he could become the "real" Lennon.

Later, in 1984, I encountered Yoko in court, when she testified in a civil suit filed by Jack Douglas, who claimed that he coproduced *Double Fantasy* and *Milk and Honey* and wanted part of the profits from Lennon's last two albums.

Many of Yoko's supporters testified on her behalf in the suit, including Jann Wenner, the founder of *Rolling Stone.* He sat through much of the testimony and even watched me complete a sketch. When he looked it over, he asked if he could buy the piece. Yoko, seeing Wenner's interest in my sketches, came up to us during a recess and bluntly stated, "All of the sketches are sold."

Since I had never spoken to her before, I wondered what she meant about the sketches. Yoko, it seemed to me, was still quite shaken by John's death and the controversy about the albums. She didn't do herself much good when she testified about the production of the albums because, I'm sorry to say, she came across like a dragon lady. I don't think she meant to, but Yoko got carried away with what she thought was the truth.

The judge, however, believed that there had been a bona fide contract with Douglas to produce the albums and awarded him three million dollars. Although Yoko had lost a major amount of money, she instructed her close friend, Eli Mintz, to request that my sketches of the case be sent to her. I had learned to cope with immediate "requests" and told Mintz that if I heard from her later, perhaps we could arrange something.

Well, one evening a week later, I received a call from Mintz asking me if I could deliver the sketches in person to Yoko at noon the next Saturday at the Dakota. I cleaned up the sketches the night before and decided to bring an old sketch I had done of John and Yoko together during the deportation hearings as a remembrance of happier times.

A Japanese woman dressed in pants answered the door of Yoko's seventh-floor apartment and ushered me into an all-white living room that overlooked Central Park's

Strawberry Fields. To the left of a window stood a rather large Egyptian mummy covered with black hieroglyphics, finished in bright gold paint and enclosed in glass, and to the right sat a white Steinway piano, which had been a gift from John to Yoko, covered with pictures of the Lennons as youngsters and their relatives. A magnificent Chinese scroll painting positioned above a modern white sofa caught my eye. I studied its ancient depth and spotted a bearded old Chinese gentleman portrayed with great dignity against a background of trees and mountains that reached into eternity.

While I gazed at the scroll, Yoko came into the room. "Hello, it is so good of you to come," she said as we kissed each other on each cheek European-style. Yoko asked me to remove my shoes, and we walked to the door, where five other pairs of shoes sat.

As tea and cake were served to us on the sofa, I unwrapped the package that contained my drawings. She picked up each one and studied it. Those, indeed, were the sketches she wanted to buy. When she held the last one, though, her hands began to shake like a leaf hit by a strong wind, and tears formed in her eyes. It was the sketch from the deportation trial. "I was pregnant with Sean," she whispered.

We talked and then walked around the living room. I pointed out a photo of a middle-aged woman who so looked like Yoko. Although her eyes weren't Oriental, the cheekbones, smile, and expression were identical. "Strange," Yoko explained, "but John always said I reminded him of the aunt who raised him." I admired another picture, one of Yoko as a little doll-like girl in a Japanese kimono, and spotted another of her family in Western-style clothes. Elizabeth Barrett Browning's original handwritten poem "How Do I Love Thee," another gift from John, hung on a nearby wall.

The apartment seemed like a museum with an eclectic gathering of items of unbelievable taste for classic design and color; each piece obviously had been carefully chosen and somehow represented a special moment in the life of the Lennons. It was obvious that Yoko still suffered from the loss of her husband, and I was pleased that she had responded so favorably to the extra sketch I brought as a present. Yoko openly talked about John, their family, and their antique-buying. Pointing to a beautiful Renoir painting, Yoko said with a smile, "That was our first joint investment."

Two of Yoko's friends sat in the kitchen talking quietly when we showed them the sketches of the trial. One friend even suggested that Yoko return the favor and give me a large ink sketch of her done and signed by John while on their honeymoon.

Yoko also showed me Sean's room, which had a lovely view of Central Park. The room was lined with shelves filled with neatly stacked toys, including robots and cars, and the bathroom—designed by young Sean—was painted in bold red and black.

Finally, Yoko played both *Double Fantasy* and *Milk and Honey* for me, and it turned out to be one of the most pleasurable private concerts I had ever experienced. The albums, which seemed to me to have a definite Japanese influence, transformed Yoko into another time and another place. She hid her face in her hands and listened to the last of her creative collaborations with John.

Yoko concluded my visit by autographing two albums for my sons and a montage used to advertise the albums for my daughter. The afternoon turned out to be an extraordinary stroll through the home and life of a worldwide legend.

The case of Jack Henry Abbott, accused of killing newlywed waiter-playwright-actor Richard Adan, is one of the most notorious and controversial, at least in my judgment, on record. The history of this incident began when Abbott, a convicted killer, read Norman Mailer's popular book *The Executioner's Song,* about the imprisonment of Gary Gilmore and his death, and wrote to Mailer to tell him that he, too, had written a book about prison life called *In the Belly of the Beast.* Mailer was so taken with Abbott's work that he not only sent it to superagent Morton Janklow but also began an international public-relations campaign for the release of the imprisoned author.

Although Abbott had stabbed a fellow inmate to death, Mailer said that no talented person, even if he had killed someone, should be in jail. Abbott's friendship with Mailer grew, and eventually Abbott's own prison book earned critical acclaim after its release by an established trade publisher. Using his international literary contacts, Mailer's effort to gain the release of Abbott was successful, and the killer again walked the streets. The publication of the book and his release from prison brought notoriety to both Abbott and Mailer, but that was nothing compared to the public outrage and to the media coverage of the Adan murder outside a New York restaurant soon after Abbott's release.

During the January 1982 trial, Mailer, who brought an entourage of friends with him to court, sat in the first row on the left side of the courtroom. Judge Irving Lang allowed artists to sit at tables in front of the spectator section. That was an ideal situation because I literally sat right behind Jack Henry Abbott.

A tall and gaunt white man with Oriental eyes, Abbott looked dangerous and distrusting. There was something about him that immediately frightened me; if I saw a man like him walking down the street, I'd probably cross the street so I wouldn't have to pass by him. Later in the trial, I literally shook when Abbott said that he wanted to see my sketches of him.

The trial generated many tense and dramatic moments. The first came when a young theater student stood up, looked around the courtroom, and pointed at Abbott as the man he saw stab Richard Adan. Abbott held his head down and didn't look up until well after the identification.

Defense attorney Ivan Fisher had urged Abbott himself to testify on his own behalf, and Abbott did himself in while reading sections from his book. Although *The New York Times* had called the book "awesome, brilliant," I regarded what I heard in court as bone-chilling and disgusting. Somehow I couldn't believe the book was a work of art when you heard from the author's lips the joy he got in seeing a man killed by his own hand:

> You've slipped out the knife, eight-to-ten-inch blade, double edge. You see the spot. It's a target between the second and third button on his shirt. A light pivot toward him with your right shoulder and the world turns upside down. . . . A knife is an intimate weapon. Very personal. It unsettles the mind because you are not killing in physical self-defense, you are killing to live respectably in prison. It's like cutting into hot butter, no resistance at all. They always whisper one thing at the end: 'Please.' You get the odd impression he is not imploring you not to harm him but to do it right. You leave him in the blood staring with dead eyes.

Abbott also read still another passage about how much he enjoyed seeing the blood spill out of his victim as the knife plunged into the body. Disgusting, absolutely disgusting. I could have thrown up when I heard that section of the book, but when I turned around to look at Norman Mailer, he had such a look of pride on his face. It was as if he had listened to his own son recite a poem in a classroom.

I was truly baffled by what I heard and what I saw because I couldn't see how anyone could have interest in that kind of graphic violence and murder. Perhaps it was due to the fact that I was a woman and didn't have the necessary machismo, but I couldn't see why people accepted violent death. How anyone believed that violence became an art form in Abbott's story was beyond me.

On the witness stand, Abbott roared like a lion and wept like an infant. His emotions swung from anger and arrogance to pride and remorse about Adan. He said that he didn't intend to kill Adan, that his death was a tragic mistake, a terrible misunderstanding. When Abbott walked into a restaurant on the Bowery called Binibon's, he said Adan looked at him improperly. But Abbott asked him where the men's room was anyway, and Adan told Abbott he would have to go outside. When he did, Abbott said he saw Adan and thought he, Abbott, was going to be harmed.

With that testimony, Henry Howard, the father-in-law of the victim, screamed, cursed, and shrieked his anger at Abbott from the gallery. The whole court was shaken by the incident, and I thought the judge might declare a mistrial. However, he decided to continue the proceedings, and the entire room was tense, especially during further testimony by the defendant.

We also heard testimony about Abbott's pathetic past—about being beaten in jail, about being starved, about being kept in solitary confinement during all his years in prison.

On the second day of the jury's deliberations, which also was Abbott's thirty-eighth birthday, the five men and seven women of the jury marched back into the courtroom with a verdict. I could tell by the look on their faces that there must have been serious disagreement and hard discussion in the jury room. Nonetheless, Abbott was found guilty. The whole day seemed rather macabre because Mailer had earlier brought a birthday cake to Abbott in jail and carried what appeared to be a present into the courtroom when the jury rendered its decision.

Judge Lang later told Abbott, who had already spent twenty-four years in prison, that he was a violent and persistent offender and sentenced him to a twenty-three-years-to-life jail term. Norman Mailer created a stir in the courtroom when he said in a manner loud enough for most people to hear, "That's a killing sentence."

The full impact of the trial and of the verdict didn't hit Mailer until the proceedings ended. Outside the courtroom I heard a saddened Mailer tell the press, "My judgment was imperfect."

ANOTHER NOTORIOUS CASE TOOK PLACE IN 1983, WHEN GAIL Collins Pappalardi stood trial for purposely shooting in the neck and killing her husband, Felix, thirty-three, a well-known rock musician. While defense attorneys Neal Comer and Hal Meyerson tried to prove that Gail, who had written lyrics for the rock group Cream, had accidentally shot Felix, most of us in court focused on the "open" marriage the couple shared and the extracurricular sex that was common for both spouses and the live-in lovers they shared.

This case generated a great deal of interest with legal, media, and women's rights groups, and the courtroom was mobbed every day. Gail didn't bat an eyelash about all the testimony concerning kinky sex. Quite the opposite: She read intimate passages from her diary that revealed how bizarre her marriage and her sexual relationships had become.

Wearing a purplish sweater draped over her shoulder and with her blond hair curled on each side and parted in the middle, Gail sobbingly told the court that Felix enjoyed three-way sex. He would have sex with a woman, turn the woman over to Gail, and then have sex with Gail. Norma May, a woman who had lived with the Pappalardis in that sexual arrangement for six years, confirmed Gail's testimony and called it "a magnificent relationship."

Gail, between sobs, also told the court that Felix often didn't return home until five in the morning, saying that he spent most of the night at The Ritz, an East Village rock spot. But, claimed Gail, he really was with his mistress, Valerie Merrians. The woman once even called Gail to tell her she was going to commit suicide unless she could have Felix on Tuesdays and Fridays. However, it was okay if Gail kept Felix at home the rest of the week. "I told Valerie," Gail testified, "that Felix would never go for it."

Felix's sister, Celia Tardibono, also testified about a phone conversation she had with Gail some three months before the shooting. The women discussed the trouble they had with their husbands, and the defense attorneys had a field day with the woman.

"Do you think that Mrs. Pappalardi would have killed Felix and confided in you about the troubles?" asked Hal Meyerson. "She certainly listened to your troubles with your husband. Do you have any personal interest in telling the court about Mrs. Pappalardi? Certainly, you are the only sister or sibling in the family, and you would eventually be heir to the estate."

The prosecution then put on the stand a gun expert who testified that the butt of the derringer used in the shooting was no longer than a man's thumb, which would make it awkward to use accidentally.

In response to those statements, one of the defense attorneys picked up the weapon used in the killing and "accidentally" pulled the trigger of the unloaded gun. "Oops, sorry," he said. Needless to say, the judge wasn't amused by the theatrics and admonished the lawyer.

But he had proved his point. Hearing the hammer of the gun snap in court was not only quite frightening but also effective. It showed how easily the gun could have gone off.

Later Gail took the stand again and said that Felix had tried to show her how to use the gun and had insisted that she practice loading and shooting it. "I pulled the hammer back and then something happened," she stated. "To this day, I don't know what happened. Everything was a fog."

She faced a twenty-five-year prison sentence and the

loss of a quarter-million-dollar inheritance if found guilty of murdering her husband. Fortunately for Gail, the jury found her not guilty. Although I was shocked by the verdict, perhaps the jury believed Gail when she earlier begged them to understand, "I didn't mean to kill him. It was an accident."

The 1976 trial of the two men charged with kidnapping Sam Bronfman, son of Edgar, the internationally known head of the Seagram's liquor empire and one of the wealthiest men in the world, proved to be both dramatic to cover and a royal pain to attend. Held in the courthouse in White Plains, I got up every morning at five, took the six o'clock train to Penn Station, a cab to Grand Central Station, and another train to White Plains.

When I got to the courthouse, I fought a long line of people to get into the place. Fortunately, I always managed to obtain an excellent seat, where I could see the jury, the Bronfman family, and the men accused of the kidnapping. One defendant, Dominic Byrne, who was nicknamed "The Good Little Leprechaun," wore glasses and a mustache and always smiled. That smile and those blue eyes, which always twinkled, were quite captivating. Mel Lynch, whose car was traced to the ransom payoff, was the other defendant. He had worked as a fireman in Brooklyn for twelve years.

Sam Bronfman, a precise and very matter-of-fact kind of man, told the court about his ordeal in a nonemotional manner. He said he had been given sandwiches and soda throughout his time in captivity, but Lynch had been hard on him while Byrne was nice. However, Bronfman stated that his captors had threatened him with death many times. He also verified other facts concerning his kidnapping: how a gun was held to his back, and identification of the clothes he wore during the incident.

Then the big day came. Sam's father, billionaire Edgar Bronfman, testified. He brought a large number of people with him, including his new wife, who was quite visibly pregnant. Edgar, a haughty man, stated that the ransom note asking for four million six hundred thousand dollars had been delivered to him lacking ten cents' postage. Detailing his location on a map given to him by the prosecution, Edgar also explained that a man wearing a stocking mask collected the ransom, which was one-half of the original amount, and drove off. However, Sam was not released for two more days and not without excellent work by New York detectives.

I wasn't too pleased when Edgar tried to throw his weight around and stop me from drawing in the courtroom. During a recess his public-relations man approached me and flatly stated that Bronfman didn't want to be sketched. Well, of course, I made believe that I didn't hear him and went about my work. When I finished the sketch, Bronfman looked down his nose at me in a most unpleasant manner, as if I and my job as a courtroom artist were beneath his status. Edgar, incidentally, later obtained one of my sketches of him at a get-together with other prominent people. NBC's John Chancellor asked me for the piece and then turned it over to Bronfman.

The rumors surrounding this case were extensive and vicious. One story emphasized that the ransom money reportedly given to Lynch and Byrne, Irishmen with marked Irish brogues, would have been funneled into the Irish Republican Army to support its violence campaign against the British. Another story suggested that Sam's mother, Ann Margaret Loev Bronfman, had been involved in nontraditional sexual liaisons.

Finally, though, the defense argued that Lynch and Sam Bronfman had been homosexual lovers and had "reluctantly" participated in a phony kidnapping that had been engineered by the Seagram heir himself. Lynch told the court that he met Bronfman at his mother's estate in Purchase, New York, on August 8, 1975, to plan the hoax.

Other crucial evidence also was introduced, including a cassette recorder and part of a book, *83 Hours to Dawn,* a story about the Barbara Jane Mackle kidnapping in Georgia. The ransom note sent to Edgar closely resembled passages of the Mackle ransom note printed in the book.

The testimony against Sam Bronfman's version of the kidnapping piled up, and the prosecution didn't even recall Sam to clear up the confusion. It seemed as if Lynch's Irish-accented statements closed the case.

Later the jury agreed with what everyone in court believed happened: Samuel Bronfman probably engineered his own kidnapping for financial and other gain. Lynch and Byrne were found not guilty.

IN 1982, NBC NEWS SENT ME TO NEWPORT, RHODE Island, to cover the trial of Klaus Von Bulow on charges of attempted murder of his wife, "Sunny." She was hospitalized at Columbia Presbyterian in New York City, suffering from an irreversible coma, in which she had been for approximately thirteen months. Before leaving for Newport, I swung down to the hospital to sneak a peak into Sunny's room. As I waited in the hallway, several nurses went into the room and opened the door enough for me to obtain a good view of Sunny; I saw enough to re-create the scene from memory for a good sketch for NBC.

I flew up to Newport and took a taxi to a motel across the street from the courthouse. It seemed as if every press organization in the country sent a reporter to cover the trial, and all of them stayed at this lodge. The next morning I met Jim Van Sickle, the reporter with whom I worked so hard on the Jean Harris trial, in the motel coffee shop for breakfast. Jim quickly pointed out that Von Bulow also was eating in the restaurant. With the defendant of the case so close to me, I ran up to the room, got my art supplies, and decided to go for a good close-up of the man. Von Bulow was an excellent subject, although he occasionally lowered his head.

When I finished the portrait, Jim and our field producer suggested I show the sketch to Klaus. I immediately questioned whether I had the nerve to approach Von Bulow, but decided it would be interesting to chat with him. Although I had already noticed his aristocratic look, partial bald head, blue eyes, and rather sharp nose, I wanted to get a close-up view of Klaus at the table.

I figured brief introductions always were best, so I asked him if he wanted to see my drawing. Von Bulow asked me to sit down, and he talked in a patronizing manner about art and his appreciation of it, as if I were an artistic illiterate. If Von Bulow were the least bit concerned about his guilt, it didn't show in the face I saw and sketched.

However, his expression and voice changed when I showed him the sketch I had done of him. "This is very, very good," he said, as a broad smile brought out laugh lines on his face. If his eyes were his hands, he would have quickly helped himself to my sketch.

When I noticed he had become uncomfortable because other people were staring at us with a "Who is that woman?" curiosity, I folded my sketchbook, went back to my own table, and gobbled down my breakfast.

There was a regal air about Von Bulow in court. I didn't like it. He looked at me, at reporters, and at spectators as though he regarded us as beneath him. I immediately noticed Sunny's daughter, Ala Kneissil, from her first marriage, to Prince Von Auersperg. An attractive woman dressed elegantly, she testified quite beautifully and cheerfully about her love for her mother. She also told the court that she had instructed her mother not to leave Klaus.

It was only after Sunny went into a coma and her brother showed her a black bag with a needle that had contained insulin that Ala suspected Klaus of any wrongdoing.

She provided dramatic testimony, and the defense attorney couldn't move her on any of her recollections of her mother prior to her hospitalization. In the meantime, Klaus looked down, with his jaw tightly clenched. You could see he thought things weren't going well for him.

Although I had obtained some excellent sketches of Von Bulow and of several witnesses, I unfortunately missed several key players in the case. They were Maria ("Schrilli") Schrallhammer, the maid who found the black bag; Dr. Richard Stock, the family doctor; and actress Alexandra Iles, the "other woman" in Klaus's life. Iles, in particular, did a number on Von Bulow because she stated how deeply they loved each other and how deeply they wanted to be married. That, perhaps, established the motive for injecting Sunny with a harmful dose of insulin.

The outcome of the case was disastrous for Von Bulow. The jury found him guilty. It was an unfortunate affair for me professionally. My sketches never made the air. True, television cameras had been allowed in the courtroom, but the crews weren't permitted to film the jury, which I sketched.

After the end of the trial, I received a call from an independent producer for public television who wanted to use my sketches in a piece he was putting together on cameras versus artists in the courtroom. NBC okayed the release of the Von Bulow material, and I shipped it out to the producer.

An assistant to the producer called later and informed me she had left my sketches in a taxi. Therefore, they wouldn't be used on the program or returned to me. In the end, Klaus Von Bulow appealed and won his case, and I received a small insurance check for my precious but lost sketches.

HOWEVER, I COULDN'T COMPLAIN THAT MUCH. FOR EVERY catastrophe I went through in the news business, there also seemed to be a highlight. A few years before the Von

Bulow case, I covered the trial of Paula Ramsey, a Haitian woman accused, along with her brother, of kidnapping designer Calvin Klein's daughter Marci. Hired as a babysitter, Ramsey twisted facts to suit her own advantage in a crazy defense that included claims that Klein had made numerous passes at her.

Klein, a good father, had fallen prey—like so many other prominent people—to evildoers who thought nothing of harming a child to extort money from a loving parent. It seemed to me that application of the so-called Lindbergh Rule, which provides for the death of kidnappers, was the only way to prohibit such cruel and indiscriminate acts.

Fortunately, the jury rendered a guilty verdict against Ramsey and her brother, which hopefully had some impact on preventing celebrity kidnap attempts of any kind. And during the trial a writer for *TV Guide* sat next to me and completed a story that called me "one of the most prominent practitioners of this obscure, fascinating craft, courtroom illustration."

Quick Sketches

In 1983 I covered a hearing in Supreme Court in Manhattan that brought model/actress Brooke Shields, then eighteen, and her mother into court over a disagreement about who owned and controlled nude photographs taken of Brooke as a child. Photographer Gary Gross retained Richard Golub, the husband of actress Marisa Berenson, for the case. His wife appeared in court several times, and she and Brooke in the same courtroom made the place glow, especially since the outcome seemed so predictable.

Mother Teri Shields had signed a valid and a proper contract for the picture session.

Although Brooke lost the court case, I genuinely felt she won the courtroom beauty contest. True, Marisa was a most attractive woman, but a real beauty she wasn't, and she didn't fit into the same field with Brooke.

To me, Marisa's beauty seemed reconstructed. She had a perfect nose, long and curly brown hair, and very beautiful eyes. But Marisa was painfully thin, almost anorexically thin. Although she seemed very, very charming, I got the feeling there was something very synthetic about her. On the other hand, Brooke looked absolutely gorgeous and seemed so natural. Maybe that was it; Brooke radiated beauty as well as comfortableness.

WHEN I SKETCHED JOHN PHILLIPS, THE FOUNDER OF THE 1960s rock group The Mamas and the Papas, in 1980 in federal court on a seven-count indictment for conspiracy to sell ten thousand illegal pills and cocaine, he looked absolutely pathetic and pleaded guilty. Unsteady on his feet and wearing rumpled clothes, Phillips looked and acted as if he were totally wacked out of his mind on one or several illegal substances. It was spooky watching the man.

In addition to being so sketetal-looking, he didn't seem to have any mental focus of what he had done to himself and even told the judge he was drug-free. Neither I nor anyone else in the courtroom could have believed that this ghost of a man had dealt with his addiction problems.

SYDNEY BIDDLE BARROWS, THE INFAMOUS *MAYFLOWER* Madam who ran a high-class house of flesh in New York City, may have gotten caught and driven out of one profession, but she sure knew how to parlay her business sense into big dollars when she sold book and movie rights. Although I'm from a conservative bedroom community and a wife, mother, and grandmother, I covered her trial in 1984 with great interest because Sydney was a local Monmouth (New Jersey) County girl.

Like thousands of other readers, I bought her book because I didn't comprehend how a woman with her porcelainlike face, perfect skin, beautiful features, and socialite background became a madam. Like her or not, Barrows knew how to turn a buck.

ONE OF THE SADDEST DAYS I EVER SPENT IN A COURTROOM was covering the 1978 pretrial appearance of punk rocker Sid Vicious of the Sex Pistols. While on drugs he apparently had killed his girlfriend with a knife. Many fellow punkers, dressed in the strangest manner and wearing the craziest hairdos, attended the hearing. They didn't seem to have any direction whatsoever. The one thing they seemed to have in common with Sid was that they were such lost souls.

The judge was going to deny bail to Vicious, who was so thin that it appeared he suffered from the bone condition osteoporosis, but smart legal debate by the defense attorney won out. Vicious was released from jail, and the very next day he overdosed on drugs and died. It was hard for me to have anything but compassion for someone who had so pathetically lost his way in life.

ON THE OTHER HAND, ONE OF THE MOST COMICAL SITUATIONS I ever witnessed in a courtroom involved entertainer Woody Allen. He had brought a civil suit in 1984 against a man to prohibit him from doing public impersonations of him. When I entered the courtroom and sat in the jury box to sketch the scene, I saw the door to the judge's chambers ajar and spotted the real Woody Allen. This was a classic situation and showed how life sometimes imitates art: Allen appeared to be having a panic attack and quickly closed the door to the courtroom.

Choosing not to confront the impersonator or the judge in the courtroom, Allen stayed out of sight while his attorney argued that the impersonator's activities, especially selling items on television commercials, embarrassed the performer. The impersonator, meanwhile, took the whole thing in stride as he sat quietly at the defendant's table until the judge ruled that he would have to find another means to make a living.

DURING THE 1985 TAX EVASION TRIAL INVOLVING BOXING promoter Don King, the ever-flamboyant defendant fascinated me from an artistic standpoint. I had seen him on television and had immediately recognized him because of his hairdo. His hair stood straight up on his head, as if he had had an electric shock.

I sketched him in the courtroom and suddenly he turned around to me and said, "Rembrandt." Never before had such a single-word quote meant so much to me. Rembrandt always had been one of my favorite artists, and *The New York Times* even mentioned King's reference to me in its story about the case. Incidentally, it was a challenge to draw the man's hair. It flowed straight up in the air, while his mustache curled down. He wore long sideburns and little, wispy hair hung from his chin, which almost gave King the appearance of having a goatee.

POOR YUL BRYNNER. HE SHOWED UP IN COURT LOOKING awful from his fight against cancer, but he testified anyway in his suit against a famous New York restaurant, charging that he became ill with trichinosis from eating pork spareribs. In my mind, however, I couldn't erase the image of the actor prancing around the stage in knee-high, silk knickers and pointed, gold headdress as the lead character in *The King and I.* Even as I sketched Brynner in a business suit, I noticed he had an Oriental look to his eyes. The lawsuit was settled out of court for a reported three million dollars, but Yul didn't have the opportunity to enjoy the money because cancer claimed his life a short time later. I felt badly that a man who was so sick to begin with had to expend some of his energy in the last days of his life talking about trichinosis.

VICTORIA SELLERS, DAUGHTER OF THE LATE ACTOR PETER Sellers, appeared in federal court in Newark in 1986 on charges of selling cocaine. Her conviction wasn't as shocking as her physical appearance. Victoria was anything but glamorous and didn't resemble the woman who had been pictured in the buff in an issue of *Playboy*.

In the magazine spread Victoria wore a blond wig, false eyelashes, and every imaginable facial makeup. In court I hardly recognized her as a plain Jane who wore little makeup, a red jacket, and a white skirt.

A LETTER WRITTEN BY MARILYN MONROE WHILE IN A PSYchiatric hospital to acting coach Lee Strasberg, and the court battle about who legally owned the letter, brought out some of the most fascinating Hollywood history and gossip I had ever heard. The letter, allegedly found in a garbage can by someone who had worked for Lee, had been put on the auction block after Lee's death, and his wife, Anna, sought to keep the piece in the family estate.

Anna, an attractive woman who seemed intensely loyal to her family and heritage, testified that she didn't want the letter auctioned for a reserve price of eighteen thousand five hundred dollars because it was a personal and confidential piece of correspondence to her late husband from his most famous pupil.

The Monroe letter also had personal significance to Anna because she found Marilyn's correspondence at the same time she discovered a letter to Lee from actress Joan Crawford, proposing marriage. Both letters found their way into Anna's hands two weeks before she married Lee.

* * *

THE 1984 LIBEL CASE THAT PITTED GENERAL WILLIAM Westmoreland, the former commander of our forces in Vietnam, against CBS for a *60 Minutes* report about enemy troop strength and our own buildup, brought an incredible cast of witnesses, including former Johnson administration officials, military men, and intelligence officers. However, I was most impressed by Westmoreland. He truly seemed personally and professionally hurt by the report, and he appeared to stake his integrity and his dignity as a military commander on whether he could prove that he had never inflated the enemy troop count for political or other purposes.

As he testified, I found him animated, and his face took on an aura of mystery because his deep-set eyes brought a feeling of darkness to his face. But he sat erect and spoke clearly. He said he had been "rattlesnaked" and deceived during the making of the 1982 report into believing it would be about the enemy's infamous Tet Offensive of 1968. Westmoreland not only characterized the interview as an "inquisition" but also said, "I was participating in my own lynching, but the problem was I didn't know what I was being lynched for."

At one point, though, the attorney for Westmoreland tried to bring some levity to the case. He asked the general if he actually licked his lips as much throughout the entire *60 Minutes* interview as shown in the televised segment. The general said that his mouth dried out since bright lights were used and the camera rolled continuously. But since the interview, Westmoreland had followed his wife's instructions to use Chap Stick when talking to reporters to avoid the dryness and to avoid the appearance of nervousness.

I felt sorry for Mike Wallace, the reporter on the story. He seemed to be ill much of the time, and his face was deeply drawn and lined. But I tried to cheer him up once outside the courtroom when I related how I used to call his son (a correspondent for NBC News) Mike instead of Chris, and how Chris called me Freda (the name of my twin sister, then an illustrator for ABC News) instead of Ida.

ON A SPECIAL ASSIGNMENT FOR *SPORTS ILLUSTRATED* I covered the 1986 antitrust suit the USFL brought against the prestigious NFL. I thought the most exciting testimony of the proceedings came from none other than Howard Cosell. Although I had heard his sports reports on radio and seen his work on television, he was more than I thought he would be in real life. What a character! He was the most knowledgeable man I had ever been exposed to in terms of sports, and he certainly could have given lessons on assertiveness. The sparring between attorney Frank Rothman, who represented the NFL, and Cosell, who testified on behalf of the USFL, was the highlight of the trial.

As a matter of fact, it probably was the single best performance of any witness I had covered in my career. Cosell testified for four hours, and his comments were laced with humor, sarcasm, bombasts, and anger. All were delivered in a loud, positive manner, and the sportscaster changed moods several times, from sedate storyteller to wounded bull.

At one point Rothman said to Cosell, "If I ask you a question that you don't understand, you stop me." Howard shot back, "If you ask me a question that I don't understand, you will have the biggest story of the century."

As Howard Cosell completed his testimony, he walked past the press section and said, "That was some performance." It was. Although he was seated throughout his testimony to the court, Cosell provided an outstanding stand-up comic routine.

When a charity later asked me to donate a piece of my artwork to be auctioned off, I immediately thought of a Cosell sketch. My husband said, "Who will buy a sketch of Howard Cosell? You better donate something with it." So I chose a floral watercolor, which I also matted, framed, and donated to the charity.

The night of the auction I learned that the Cosell sketch was purchased for one thousand dollars and the watercolor for only three hundred fifty dollars.

The trial of David "Son of Sam" Berkowitz, above with attorneys Ira Jultack and Leon Stern, changed my view of the criminal justice system. I realized that capital punishment might be justified in certain cases.

During the Mob Commission trial, Carmine Persico stood before Judge Richard Owen and acted as his own attorney. Codefendants Gennaro Langella, Anthony Indelicato, Ralph Scopo, Christopher Furnari, Anthony Salerno, Anthony Corallo, and Anthony Santoro watched his performance.

U.S. Assistant District Attorney Walter Mack made his opening statement in the trial of Paul Castellano and the Gambino family. Soon after I sketched Castellano, the mob chieftain was found shot to death.

An undercurrent of intimidation filled Judge Eugene Nickerson's courtroom during the trial of John Gotti and six codefendants on racketeering and conspiracy charges.

Tomasso Bushetta described the inner workings of Sicilian and American organized-crime activities during the Pizza Connection trial.

Accused of taking part in the criminal activities of the Bonanno family, defendants (right to left) Anthony Rabito, Antonio Tomasulo, Vincent Lopez, Nicolas Santoro, and Benjamin Ruggerio listened to the testimony of "Donnie Brasco," the FBI infiltrator, Joseph Pistone.

The country learned about secret contributors to Richard Nixon's 1972 presidential campaign during the Watergate-related trial of John Mitchell and Maurice Stans. The defendants watched attorney Peter Fleming question New Jersey politician Harry Sears.

I sketched Ayatollah Khomeini in 1976 in the Kabul, Afghanistan, airport. The Muslim leader, who then lived in exile in Paris, politely conversed in French with me and showed no hostility for America.

Former Yippie leader Abbie Hoffman entertained his followers in 1980 outside the courtroom but turned serious when he stood before Judge Milton Williams on charges of selling cocaine and jumping bail.

Nancy and Henry Kissinger listened incredulously to the testimony of Ellen L. Kaplan, a member of the militant Fusion Energy Foundation, who had provoked a confrontation with the couple at Newark International Airport.

John Zacarro, shown in court before Judge George Roberts with Assistant District Attorney Seth Rosenberg and defense attorney Arthur Liman, stayed cool during his appearances on fraud charges.

G. Gordon Liddy, one of the Watergate "plumbers," showed no remorse about his lead role in the hotel break-in during a court appearance prior to his 1977 release from a federal correctional facility.

Kathy Boudin, Judith Clarke, Sam Brown, and Dave Gilbert, bruised and disheveled after being in a car accident, were arraigned in Nyack, New York, on robbery and murder charges in the Brinks case.

A defendant known as Africa appeared in court during the controversial trial of the MOVE group in Philadelphia.

Jackie Kennedy Onassis sat with her daughter, Caroline, during a 1983 case involving paparazzo photographer Ron Galella. The former first lady was the most dignified personality I sketched during my fifteen-year courtroom career.

Yoko Ono, still shaken from the death of John Lennon, was involved in a breach of contract suit brought by record producer Jack Douglas in 1984. She listened as Judge Martin Stecher received the verdict from the jury, which awarded three million dollars to Douglas.

During his trial for murder, Jack Henry Abbott read passages from his book, *In the Belly of the Beast,* and prosecutor James H. Fogel listened to a bone-chilling account of a stabbing.

Brooke Shields lost a court battle with photographer Gary Gross for ownership of negatives that showed her nude. The photos were taken when Shields was ten years old.

Socialite Sidney Biddle Barrows, the "Mayflower Madam," first entered a plea of not guilty on a charge of operating a posh prostitution service.

Ivan Boesky, flanked by prosecutor Charles Carberry and defense attorneys, pleaded guilty to one charge of insider trading.

David Crosby provided a graphic example of how drugs physically and creatively destroy talented entertainers. The former Crosby, Stills, and Nash member had been addicted to cocaine.

Mick Jagger of the Rolling Stones seemed awkward in court as he testified in a suit that resulted in the dismissal of his business manager.

Howard Cosell delivered a great comic performance, and he and Donald Trump, former owner of the New Jersey Generals, also gave lessons in assertiveness during the antitrust trial that pitted the United States Football League against the National Football League.

In a libel suit against CBS, General William Westmoreland stated that he had been "rattlesnaked" by *60 Minutes* in a report about the Vietnam War. Israeli General Ariel Sharon, who had brought a separate libel action against *Time* for a story about the massacre of Palestinians in refugee camps, was animated and positive in his testimony.

Detective Jerry Giorgio, who had investigated the death of violinist Helen Mintiks at the Metropolitan Opera House, testified against accused killer Craig Crimmins. I won a second Emmy for my work during this trial.

Jean Harris appealed to the jury for a favorable verdict during her trial for the murder of Dr. Herman Tarnower, who developed the Scarsdale Diet.

Mark David Chapman, who had admitted during his arraignment that he killed John Lennon and had been remanded to Bellevue Hospital, read a passage from *Catcher in the Rye* at a sentencing hearing. Chapman's attorney claimed his client had lost considerable weight because he had refused to eat after fellow inmate David "Son of Sam" Berkowitz told Chapman the food was poisoned.

Judge Burton Roberts called David Bullock "a monster and a viper" when he sentenced him to 150 years in prison for killing five men and one woman.

Irwin Margolies, implicated in the murder of three CBS employees, looked beaten when Adair identified him as the mastermind of a plot that also involved the killing of a witness against him in a separate federal fraud case.

With his face scratched and a finger on his left hand bandaged, Robert E. Chambers, Jr., stood defiantly before Judge Richard B. Lowe and was arraigned in the murder of Jennifer Dawn Levin.

Bernhard Goetz, the subway vigilante who shot four young men on a New York City subway, listens to the testimony of one of the victims, Troy Canty. Photographs of the other three are displayed by defense attorney Barry Slotnick.

I sketched John W. Hinckley, Jr., on the opening day of his trial for the attempted murder of President Reagan and press secretary James R. Brady. The legal strategy used in the case of Hinckley—and other misfits—created controversy.

Hermine Braunsteiner Ryan, accused of whipping many inmates to death in a Nazi concentration camp, frequently smirked when witnesses testified against her. She sat beside her husband, an ex-G.I., during extradition hearings.

When Massachusetts Governor Michael Dukakis posthumously pardoned Nicola Sacco in 1977, NBC News gave me a special assignment: to re-create the infamous Sacco-Vanzetti trial of the 1920s, which included a sketch of the defendants in a prisoner's cage.

Edwin Wilson, the "merchant of death," who was arrested in Kennedy International Airport, listened to testimony against him in federal court, where he was charged with illegally running arms to Libya.

The Reverend Sun Myung Moon, leader of the Unification Church, was found guilty of tax evasion in federal court.

One of the most bizarre cases I covered involved the 1979 murder of Congressman Leo Ryan and two NBC employees at an airport in Guyana. Larry Layton, a lieutenant under Jim Jones of the People's Temple, was arrested and charged with the crimes in Georgetown, Guyana.

When J. Seward Johnson died, his six children jumped into a court fight for his estate. Seward left a half-billion-dollar award to Basia (Barbara) Johnson, his third wife, and the children hung out the family dirty laundry in their challenge of the will. Basia (left) listened to Marty Richards, a Broadway producer and husband of Mary Lea, the eldest Johnson daughter, testify about the Johnson estate.

Dr. Howard Bellin, a plastic surgeon, contemplates the drawing of a patient's slightly off-center belly button. She sued him for his miscalculation, and the jury awarded $854,219 in damages to the plaintiff.

Mary Beth Whitehead pleaded for the return of "her" daughter during the dramatic Baby M case.

Adela Holtzer, who was convicted on a fraud charge, reportedly hadn't paid attorney Roy Cohn for his work. In jail, Holtzer became friends with convicted murderer Jean Harris.

SIX

Social Misfits

JUDGE BURTON ROBERTS, A MAN WHO DIDN'T MINCE WORDS with defendants or anyone else, once described for me the Criminal Court Building in Manhattan. He called it "the cesspool of humanity" and "the toilet of the city," and his courtroom demeanor reflected that viewpoint when dealing with social misfits. Although he brought understanding and compassion to his courtroom, he spoke candidly to all criminals, especially repeat offenders.

He also handed out a tough brand of justice. I respected him for that because of the vast number of defendants I saw admit to horrible, truly horrible, crimes against innocent bystanders. At times the testimony of misfits made you question whether they should be regarded as human beings. In all my life I never dreamed that men and women could kill, could maim, and could torture in such a calculated and cold-blooded manner.

Of the many misfits I covered in New York City courts, the case involving Craig Crimmins, the man arrested and charged with the 1980 murder of a woman violinist whose body had been found at the bottom of a ventilation shaft in the Metropolitan Opera House at Lincoln Center, shocked me and the city. I was first made aware of the murder after I had sketched the conviction of Senator Harrison A. Williams, Jr., in an Abscam trial. I called the assignment desk, thinking I'd head home on the next train, but an editor ordered me to grab the first cab to Criminal Court in Manhattan, where Crimmins was to be arraigned.

I found the courtroom packed with reporters, artists, and police detectives. When Crimmins and his attorney appeared before the judge, the first thing I noticed was that the defendant looked like he had come out of an alcohol or drug binge. Wearing a torn, rust-colored T-shirt and blue jeans, Crimmins looked totally out of it.

When Judge Bernard J. Fried asked Crimmins if he pleaded guilty or innocent to the murder of Helen Hagnes Mintiks at the Metropolitan Opera House, attorney Robert Ellis didn't let his client respond. "He is absolutely stunned by the events," Ellis said, "and he pleads not guilty. It would be illegal and a violation of fundamental constitutional rights for the police to interrogate my client or any client after he has asked for or retained counsel."

The judge listened intently to the attorney but denied Crimmins permission to meet privately with his father and brother, remanded him without bail to Rikers Island, and granted the attorney's request to keep his client segregated from other prisoners.

I will never forget that day because after the arraignment my reporter, Heather Bernard, and I went to the Metropolitan Opera House, where we were briefed on the killing by the Chief of Detectives Richard J. Nicastro. He told us that Helen Mintiks had disappeared during an intermission of a performance by the Berlin Ballet. After questioning 350 performers, Nicastro said an eyewitness had seen the woman enter an elevator with a man and that a police artist had drawn a composite of Crimmins, an opera house employee. He also said that a paper napkin stained with semen and a tampon were found in the opera house and both had been sent to a crime laboratory for analysis to determine blood types and any other identifying information.

I was later sent to the memorial service for Mintiks. Her friends and her fellow musicians related personal stories about Helen's grace and gentleness, and the words and the mood of the service brought tears to me as I sketched the church scene. It was such a great loss. As I learned, Mintiks had been a child prodigy and a trusting person who took people on their word.

A young woman who worked at the opera house said that Mintiks had traveled and performed throughout the world and that many of her friends referred to her as "Miss Cheesecakes" because of her bubbly smile and the wonderful cheesecake she made.

When the trial began in 1981, Crimmins remained quiet and sat before the judge with his head bowed. But this time he was well-dressed, and his pretty college student girlfriend, Mary Ann Fennell, and his sister, Donna, sat next to him.

The prosecutor had lined up an interesting array of witnesses, from the building engineers who described the opera house's maze of corridors and staircases to psychologists who evaluated Crimmins' mental health. One witness, a woman, had been hypnotized under legal and police supervision after the murder, and recalled riding in the elevator with Mintiks and a man at nine forty-five on the evening of the killing. Apparently Mintiks had been looking for ballet star Valery Panov's dressing room because she wanted to ask Panov if he would consider working with her husband, Janis Mintiks.

But the two witnesses who stood out in my mind were police detectives Mike Struk and Jerry Giorgio. They were very animated in their testimony about how they apprehended Crimmins and about how Crimmins reacted. Struk recalled that Crimmins, when first arrested, had not told the truth about his movement act by act in the opera house.

But as the detective discussed the crime, Crimmins began to feel comfortable and related how he had met "that lady" at elevator twelve. Crimmins, after being informed that the police had found his fingerprints at the murder scene, said, "What do you want me to do, say I killed her?" Officer Giorgio responded, "No, not unless it is the truth."

Due to their honesty and their solid police work on this case, I had tremendous respect for the two detectives. In addition to police testimony, the prosecutor called to the witness stand fellow district attorney Charles Heffernan, who tape-recorded the Crimmins confession.

After testifying about his role in the case, Heffernan played the confession for the court. Crimmins, who was very nervous and fooled around with his hands, slowly described his actions the evening Mintiks was killed. "I went down to my locker room to drink some beers, and on the way down there I met a lady," he said, as Heffernan conducted the interrogation. After reading the suspect his rights, Heffernan said Crimmins initially agreed to talk to authorities without the presence of his counsel.

The detectives recounted all of Crimmins' actions that night at the opera house, and Craig said he had asked Helen in elevator twelve about her fooling around with him. She got quite angry and hit Crimmins. When she got angry, Crimmins pulled out a hammer and threatened her. Crimmins said that Mintiks then started to take her clothes off, but he instructed her to put them back on and walk up a flight of stairs. On the way up the stairs, Mintiks ran and tried to escape. Crimmins caught her. "We got to the roof, and I did not know which of the doors went outside. I held her hand, and I opened one door. We went out and sat right by the pipe," Crimmins said in his videotaped confession, which was presented in court by the prosecution.

"She was trying to make conversation, asking if I worked there and if I was afraid I could not get out of there. . . . I tied her with a rope. I told her I would leave her. I would call somebody and tell them she was there. I left her there, walked back toward the door, and stood there thinking, what if she gets out of it? I heard something rattling, and I saw her with her feet undone, and she ran to the pipe and sat on it. I ran over to her, jumped over the pipe, caught her, and took her back to the same spot. I think there was a bucket there with rags in it."

When police asked if Mintiks wore shoes, Crimmins said, "I remember I took them off and tossed them away so that if she ran it would hurt her feet. I put the rags over the ropes so that it would not come loose. At that point, I picked her up and carried her up in my arms to the ledge, sat her down, and leaned her against the fan. I decided to gag her and laid her flat on her side."

The police then asked Crimmins how Mintiks' clothes had been removed. "I had my knife in the case on my belt," he stated. "I took it out and cut them off. I figured if she got loose, she would not run because she would be embarrassed.

"I decided to leave, and as I was walking away, I heard her pouncing up and down, and that's when it happened. I went back and kicked her into the shaft."

At that point, I saw Crimmins do the same thing he did at the beginning of the videotape confession: He put his hands over his mouth. The first time it seemed as if he wanted to stop himself from saying anything, but this time it appeared as if he wanted to stop the tape.

I can't believe that there was a dry eye in court after the tape was shown. My heart ached because a young talented woman's life had been snuffed out so needlessly.

The remainder of the trial was anticlimactic. The defense called Craig's mother, stepfather, and many psychologists and psychiatrists. It didn't have much impact on the jury. Craig Crimmins was found guilty of murdering Helen Hagnes Mintiks at the Metropolitan Opera House. Judge Richard Denzer later sentenced Crimmins to a twenty-years-to-life prison term and summarized the thoughts of New York City residents: "Throughout the trial, I could not help but sense a particular rage and anger about this crime."

I FOUND THE 1985 TRIAL OF BERNARD LEGEROS TO BE ONE of the most disgusting I had ever covered. Dubbed the S&M Murderer, LeGeros had been charged with killing a handsome young male model named Eigil Vesti. His body had been found by two young boys while hiking in a wooded area in Rockland County. They wandered into a smokehouse and found what at first appeared to be the body of an animal.

But police later realized that animals had ripped off the man's clothes and had eaten the flesh off of Vesti's body. But a black leather mask, which had preserved the model's face and made identification of the body easier, also provided authorities with a motive for the murder.

Police questioned Vesti's friends and family and suspected LeGeros of the sadistic crime because he seemed to know too much about the circumstances surrounding the victim's death. After further questioning by police, LeGeros stated that his boyfriend Billy Bayer had shot and killed Vesti. But LeGeros recanted his statement and confessed that he had killed the man on orders from his employer, Andrew Crispo, a New York City art gallery owner.

Crispo had once been charged with the attempted murder of an art student, who was invited to attend a party but instead was tortured and was subjected to the S&M desires of others.

The only time during the trial I saw LeGeros upset was during the testimony of Billy Bayer, who described the details that led to the murder of the male model. Crispo, LeGeros, and Bayer originally wanted to "get" the manager of the Limelight Club, Robert Rotherbell, who had insulted friends of theirs. Rotherbell didn't like the sound of the party invitation and was a no-show. Instead, the group asked Vesti. While masturbating on a sofa in an apartment where the party was being held, the group decided to go to LeGeros' country estate. Vesti later asked where he was being taken, and LeGeros and Bayer said, "You are returning to Norway in a box."

In court, Bayer identified the gun he bought for LeGeros and then described the killing. Taken into the smokehouse, Vesti was forced onto his knees, and a leather mask was placed on his face. His captors demanded that Vesti walk around them in a circle, and then Crispo allegedly shouted to LeGeros to shoot. He did.

After the jury returned a guilty verdict, Rockland County Judge Robert Meehan told LeGeros, twenty-three, that "I must protect society from you" and sentenced him to a twenty-years-to-life prison term. LeGeros, in turn, apologized to the victim's family, who had flown in from Norway for the trial, and to his own family.

John LeGeros, the defendant's father, sadly admitted, "My son is a very, very sick boy." Dr. Raquel LeGeros, a university researcher, sobbed, "My son is not a murderer. I love my son." All of us in the courtroom wished that his mother's disbelief had been the truth.

MISFITS CAME IN ALL SHAPES, SIZES, SEXES, AND AGES. IVAN Mendoza, a fifteen-year-old boy, had catapulted himself to the top of child misfits with a hideous crime when his case went to trial in 1983 under the watchful eye of Judge Burton Roberts. Mendoza had been charged with murdering eighty-eight-year-old Lena Cronenberger, who was affectionately known to neighbors as Grandma, and then raping her.

Assistant District Attorney Daniel McNulty told the court that Mendoza earned a dollar here and there for doing errands for Cronenberger and spent some time talking with the elderly woman. That was Cronenberger's fatal mistake.

McNulty then described the brutal assault on the

woman and charged that Mendoza was the only one who could have committed such an act. After being hit with a karate chop, Cronenberger was stabbed repeatedly with two knives and a carving fork. When the victim screamed, Mendoza placed a pillow over her head and slit her throat. Then he removed her clothes and raped her.

The boy made everyone in court nervous. When he wasn't concentrating on some evil place hidden deep in his mind, Mendoza's eyes shifted back and forth across the room and darted from person to person. Judge Roberts, with his power over the courtroom and street-smart insight, got Mendoza talking about karate and asked him to demonstrate his best karate chop. When he did, we all knew that this boy truly lived up to his nickname, "Ivan the Terrible."

The prosecutor also introduced evidence that physically connected Mendoza to the scene of the crime. Two hundred dollars had been stolen from Cronenberger, and Mendoza spent exactly two hundred dollars a short time after the murder at a sporting goods store. Since he never had more than a few dollars in his pocket and no visual means of support, the evidence turned out to be damning.

Later, after I showed Roberts the sketches I had done of Mendoza, he told me that the kid also had admitted to killing Louise Kong, a sixty-four-year-old woman. She, too, had been sexually assaulted, but that time Mendoza used a flashlight instead of his own penis.

The jury found "Ivan the Terrible" guilty, and Judge Roberts provided one of his characteristic admonishments as he sentenced the boy. "Mendoza's crimes are atrocious and horrendous," Roberts thundered. "What manner of boy is this? A young man who lives in a fantasy world and loves war, killings, and video games. He's a living Pac Man, eating everything that comes in front of him." The judge, citing a psychiatric report on the youth, said, "Mendoza even had sadistic fantasies of killing the detective who interrogated him after the murder."

* * *

But Mendoza seemed like a choirboy compared to Christopher Thomas, the thirty-four-year-old man responsible for the bloodiest crime in the history of New York City. Known as "Wacky" Thomas to those who dared get close enough to the man to say hello, police had jailed and then had released Thomas on a charge of attempting to rape his own mother before he began the infamous Palm Sunday Massacre that left ten people dead.

Thomas, who already had an arrest record as long as my arm on charges that included other rapes, drug possession, burglary, and attempted murder, apparently was mad at his wife, Charmane. The prosecutor said that Thomas thought that she was dating another man, Enrique Bermudes, who was the father of two of the children killed in the massacre. Thomas and Bermudes also ran a small heroin pushing operation out of Bermudes' house on Liberty Street in Brooklyn, and Mr. "Wacky" had become despondent over competitors and his deteriorating business.

The defendant sat in court listening to terrible testimony against him but didn't show any remorse whatsoever. There was nothing on his face or in his eyes that showed he regretted the slaughter of ten human beings.

As the parade of witnesses continued, the case became more frightful. A nearby baker, Carmine Rossi, testified that Bermudes hysterically approached him as he was about to enter his car; Bermudes asked if he was a policeman because his family had been shot.

The baker followed Bermudes into the house and into a nightmare that might have sprung from an Edgar Allan Poe horror scene. Rossi looked twice into the place and babbled, "my God, my God."

When he walked into another room, the baker saw "blood all over the floor. On the right side of the room, I saw a small boy about ten or twelve years old in a small bed. He was lying face down with a bullet in the back of his head. I went into the living room, and the first thing I saw was the back of the sofa. There was a woman's head leaning over it, and she had a bullet hole in her forehead. I saw a second body leaning over the back of the sofa; her face was covered with blood.

"There, on another sofa, was another body turned sideways. It started to get to me. I said to myself, 'I ain't believing what I seen.' I saw one [dead] woman who still had a glass in one hand and a sandwich in another. It looked like a wax museum. Then I heard a baby crying. She must have fallen off the lap of one of the victims. I picked up the baby and ran back to call the police. . . . It's got to be drugs. There was more going on in here than just a simple get-together. I always wondered what they were doing. There was a lot of traffic in and out."

There was no question in my mind that Thomas was a heavy drug user because, when I sketched him at his arraignment on the rape charge before the massacre, he was glassy-eyed and stared out into space. I knew he was on something, although I had no idea what substance he favored.

The prosecutor also introduced physical evidence that linked Thomas to the massacre, but the jury acquitted the man of murder and found him guilty on a lesser charge of manslaughter. I could tell from looking at the faces of the jury that there was some conflict during deliberations.

From my perspective I couldn't understand how a man who did what Thomas did—even under the influence of drugs—could be acquitted of the most vicious kind of murder.

Was that an excuse to allow someone like "Wacky" Thomas to live among decent people? I wondered how the jury and how society could find excuses for dastardly men who had a compulsion to kill, and if allowed to do so, to kill again and again and again. Thomas had such a violent record. He, like so many other misfits, was driven to the dark side of life, and they stopped living like men and became animals.

THE WHITE PLAINS TRIAL OF RICHARD HERRIN, ACCUSED of killing fellow Yale student Bonnie Garland in 1977, had less sensational testimony, but I never, never understood how a defendant could claim that another person made him "crazy" enough to "make" him commit murder. That defense has always floored me, and the way attorney Jack Litman presented it seemed like an insult to society.

Herrin, a fat man with curly hair and cold blue eyes, had been in love with Garland and was her first real boyfriend when she met him at Yale. She was seventeen years old. But young Garland loved to sing and had gone off to Europe on a Yale-sponsored choir tour, where she met another Yale man and fell in love. She wrote Herrin a "Dear Richard" letter, and he was crushed by the news.

Bonnie's mother testified that Richard called the family home the day Bonnie was expected back from Europe and asked to visit her daughter. When he came to the house, the mother noticed Herrin going into Bonnie's room with a towel over his arm. Her father, an international attorney who testified with tears in his eyes, later discovered his daughter's body and saw that her throat had been bashed in by Herrin.

You knew from watching the parents testify that Herrin also had struck a blow from which the Garlands, especially the father, would never fully recover. It was evident that Bonnie had been her daddy's girl.

When Herrin took the witness stand on his own behalf, he cried and cried like a little baby. Richard claimed that he was so pained by Bonnie's rejection, that he loved her so, that he flew into town to see if he could rekindle the love they once shared.

On the night of the murder, Herrin had carried a claw

hammer underneath the towel he brought into Bonnie's room. After she fell asleep, he bludgeoned her in the throat with the hammer, stole the Garland family car, and drove to a nearby convent. The nuns there offered him sanctuary, and two, who wore manlike suits and held hands, attended the trial. They looked at Herrin so sympathetically that I truly wondered if they thought murder was a mortal sin.

But it seemed that Herrin had support among Yale alumni and others in the Catholic Church, because more than fifty thousand dollars was raised by them for his defense. No matter how other people felt or were manipulated by Herrin, I sure couldn't find any forgiveness in my heart for that fat man with cold blue eyes.

But somehow the defense attorney had convinced the jury that Herrin's identity was so threatened by the collapse of the relationship with Bonnie that *she* triggered his violent reaction. In other words, it was Bonnie Garland who drove Richard Herrin crazy enough to kill her.

The jury found Herrin guilty of manslaughter instead of first- or second-degree murder. Although I was there in the courtroom like every member of the jury, I didn't buy the verdict. That kind of logic was offensive to me.

Years later, during a parole hearing for Herrin that I covered, Garland's parents again testified against the killer. This time, however, a slick attorney like Litman wasn't around, and the judge denied parole to a skinny and ponytailed Herrin. But like so many other misfits, Richard Herrin still wasn't in the same world with the rest of us. His eyes were wild, and the man stared off into space.

Over the years, I had covered several trials that involved what I called "kiddie criminals." There seemed something even more repugnant about these cases than many of the others because I felt we had already lost the children of a new generation. It saddened me to know that they jumped into the cesspool so early in life.

The youngest bank robber I ever met sat in Family Court in New York City munching on a candy bar. Known only as "Robert" to the media, the nine-year-old boy, who stood four feet, five inches and weighed ninety pounds, had been accused of stealing one hundred eighteen dollars from a branch of the New York Bank for Savings at gunpoint.

Dressed like an adult in a brown tweed sport coat, black tie, and off-white shirt, this kid beamed from ear to ear as defense attorney Mel Sachs told the court the little boy spent the loot on hamburgers, French fries, a movie, and a wristwatch that played a tune. Sachs said his client hadn't attended school for a year and consequently spent too much time in front of a television set, which had served as the catalyst for the boy's crime.

I started to sketch "Robert" and had a good opportunity to study him. He enjoyed the attention the robbery had brought to him. Although I doubted that television had much to do with his behavior, I sure thought this wasn't the first time he'd done something light-fingered and wondered what kind of influence his parents had on the boy.

Sachs had the gall to tell the judge that the boy didn't do anything with criminal intent. "Robert" wasn't a bank robber; he was *playing* in the bank, and the money was given to him by the cashier. The judge had little recourse and released the minirobber to the custody of his father and grandfather.

THE CASE OF THIRTEEN-YEAR-OLD ROBERT DAVIS PROVIDED a sad reminder to all of us of what might happen to children who lose their way in reckless action. A few months before he finally ended up in Bronx Supreme Court, Davis and two other boys cornered nineteen-year-old John

Hermanez on the platform of an IRT station and demanded his money. When Hermanez swung a cardboard box at the youths, a shot was fired and Hermanez lay dead on the platform.

Attorney Stanley Green towered over his baby-faced five-foot and eighty pound client and said, "The boy is not charged with pulling the trigger. One of the older boys took out the gun." Just then, a woman later identified as Hermanez's widow rocked the courtroom. "Where are they?" she screamed. "He wasn't a dog. He was a human being. You killed him." Pointing at Davis, the widow shouted sobbingly, "He's a murderer!"

Friends and relatives led the distraught woman out of the courtroom, but her screams and her sobs echoed through the hallway back into the proceedings. Judge Howard Bell fortunately set bond for Davis at five thousand dollars in spite of the attorney's plea that "He's a child and can't go anywhere. He can't take a plane to Florida." Like heck he couldn't. The kid was old enough to participate in murder and probably would do anything to avoid the penalty for it.

I also covered the first trial of a youth for murder under New York's tough new youthful offender law. Luis Bonilla, a fourteen-year-old, sat in a Bronx court accused of killing seventeen-year-old Israel Garcia for a transistor radio. The jury listened to a number of witnesses and viewed videotapes of Bonilla's statements and confessions.

With only the boy's mother showing emotion at the rendering of the verdict, the jury didn't find the kid guilty of murder, which meant he would have been sentenced as an adult and perhaps to a life sentence. Instead, the jury convicted Bonilla of manslaughter, and his case automatically reverted back to Family Court, which imposed only a three-year "restrictive placement," with parole possible after six months.

Bonilla didn't say or do anything; he stood there, looking out into space. The stout teenager didn't even look back at his mother, who was weeping into a handkerchief, or at his attorney. The judge then remanded the boy to the adolescent center on Rikers Island.

This was a landmark case in the state of New York, but it didn't work as intended. For whatever reason, juries didn't want to use the full strength of the law against youthful offenders. I believed that was terribly wrong. The kids who committed murder were already lost to a life of crime, and I thought that easy treatment of them in the courts made them believe they could beat the system and that they probably would kill again.

NOTHING DREW MORE MEDIA ATTENTION THAN A KINKY SEX and murder case, and the death of a transsexual in 1982 was no exception. Reporters packed the courtroom for the trial of Robert Ferrara and Robyn Arnold. They faced charges of shooting Ferrara's "wife," a transsexual entertainer named Diane/John Delia. Arnold, the daughter of a doctor, retained Michael Rosen, an associate of Roy Cohn. Rosen didn't come cheaply, but he was an excellent attorney and worth every penny of his fee.

Judge Harold Rothwax monitored every movement and listened to every word in the trial. Nothing slipped past him, and he rebuked prosecutor Steve Saracco for his angry cross-examinations. It appeared that Saracco wanted a fast and a certain guilty verdict.

A death threat against the key witness, Ferrara's best friend, made the case even more controversial. The witness provided the prosecutor with "letters of confession" by Ferrara, which were read in court by Saracco.

This trial seemed quite difficult for Arnold's parents. Every so often Robyn looked back at them with a "I didn't mean to do it" expression, and her father's eyes saddened. Although he held his head high, I knew that her shame in being in court on such a serious charge, which also had so many sexual implications, was his, too.

But at summations, Mike Rosen turned in a brilliant

performance that was both animated and convincing. Arnold had even inched herself away from Ferrara, as if he were a leper. On the other hand, Ferrara's attorney, who had come into the case after the defendant dumped another attorney, seemed to give up.

The jury convicted Ferrara of murder but found Arnold not guilty, and the bizarre case ended with some sort of book deal being made. I didn't know if Ferrara sidestepped the "Son of Sam" ruling, which stipulated that a murderer couldn't profit from his crime. The end of the trial seemed to be a relief to Robert Dilts, the attorney Ferrara had fired. "He sent me a nasty letter accusing me of general incompetence," Dilts said, "and he disliked me. That feeling was mutual on my part."

The attorney, who appeared as American as apple pie, seemed repulsed by the tacky, sleazy goings-on of his client. I had the feeling that every time he left the courtroom he washed his hands. I will never forget the expression on his face whenever he held a photo of Diane/John Delia; it was one of pure disgust.

THE 1980 TRIAL OF JEAN HARRIS IN WHITE PLAINS DREW international interest to Westchester County because she was accused of killing Dr. Herman Tarnower, the originator of the famous Scarsdale Diet.

For me, the trial also became a study of personality and appearance contrasts. Joel Aurnou, her lawyer, was as rock-solid and ferocious as a bulldog in his defense of Harris, whom he once characterized as a wounded bird struggling to fly. On the other side of the aisle, prosecutor George Lawrence Bolen came across as a strong believer in punishment, and Aurnou accused his counterpart of having tunnel vision in the case of Jean Harris.

My first run-in with Jean happened during the first week of the pretrial hearings. Judge Russell Leggett, a considerate and compassionate man, passed me a note and asked me to show my work to high school seniors and to explain how I sketched so quickly. I approached the students with my sketchpad, and Jean ran over to me in an agitated manner and said, "Don't show them the sketches you did of me because you drew too many wrinkles." Rather surprised by this outburst, I looked at the beautifully groomed woman, who indeed must have been most attractive in her younger years, and said, "We all fight the wrinkles."

At that moment, Jean Harris seemed so pathetic. Here the woman was charged with murder and was fighting for her life, and yet she was worried about her wrinkles.

Throughout the year-long trial, I felt that Jean didn't quite have it all together. She appeared to be a sick lady, and there was no question that she treated people, including her defense attorney, as if she knew everything and her judgment was always right. Harris, the headmistress of the posh Madeira School in McLean, Virginia, also thought she was the headmistress of the court, and I believed she thought she was the headmistress of life. Her decision was always the right one.

To me, that character flaw led to the death of Tarnower and restricted her defense in court because she wouldn't let a talented attorney do his job. The prime issue in the trial was simple: Did Harris drive to the home of her lover of fourteen years with the intent of killing him because she couldn't tolerate the idea that he had left her for a woman half her age? Or did she go there to commit suicide?

After talking to Harris' sister Virginia I decided that probably none of us will ever know what happened when Jean saw Herman. "My parents," Virginia explained, "always feared that if Jean were ever faced with a fire she might be consumed by the flames in her admiration for the vivid colors."

The description hit home and meshed with my perception of the woman. Jean truly seemed to be able to detach herself from a situation, no matter how serious, and see it only her way. I also believed that she had been raised in a social structure that taught that having material things and knowing the right people were the be-all and end-all of life. Those traits, combined with her vivid imagination, made Jean Harris a difficult woman to deal with.

Suzanne Van Derecken, a cook and housekeeper for Dr. Tarnower, took the witness stand first and described her employer's schedule of rotating Harris and Lynn Tryforos, his other lover, in and out of the house. The housekeeper also produced a little black book that contained the names of other women Tarnower entertained and what the cook fed them. It almost sounded as if Van Derecken were a madam in a house of ill repute.

Throughout the trial, Harris took a keen interest in all aspects of the case but frequently cried at the mention of Tarnower's name and the details of what happened that fateful night. Sometimes, though, she worked herself into a frenzy and lost control. She became so angry at the proceedings that she would leave the courtroom.

So many questions about Harris arose from the prosecutor's case. It was obvious that Jean had become despondent and things were getting impossible for the woman at the Madeira School. Tarnower no longer took her places or gave her gifts, but she called him frequently and once visited his home, where she found another woman's clothes in the closet. In her anger, Harris tore and shredded the clothes.

She later purchased a gun and bullets and drove to Tarnower's home early one morning. Harris claimed she went there to commit suicide, but we will never know for sure if Tarnower tried to prevent her from doing so and accidentally shot himself, or if she purposely pulled the trigger and killed him. I believed Harris when she said she had no recollection of the actual shooting; she undoubtedly forever locked that tragic moment out of her mind and her emotions.

To make matters worse for Harris, Tarnower had left her two hundred thousand dollars in his last will and testament. If she lost the trial, she would lose the inheritance.

The jury found Harris guilty of murder before I could give her several sketches that she had wanted to send to her mother. After the verdict, I read in the newspapers that Jean had become depressed and had started a hunger strike. So I called Joel Aurnou and told him I had several sketches, particularly one of Jean with her sons, that might cheer her up. He thought a visit by me was a good idea and later said, "Ida, it's the first time I've seen her smile. I'll be in New York tomorrow morning and will pick you up."

When we arrived at Valhalla, New York, Correctional Facility, I realized how much damage Jean had done to her own case by dictating to Aurnou a defense that inadvertently established a motive for the crime she was accused of committing. I had never seen a defense attorney that visibly frustrated during a trial.

"Joel," she said sadly as we walked into the visitation room, "I should have never read the Scarsdale letter in court." Aurnou, always kind and supportive of his client, said, "Don't worry about it, Jean. It showed how much you loved him [Tarnower]."

Harris embraced me and thanked me for coming. Aurnou had chosen the sketches we'd brought to prison from among the 150 or so I did during the trial, but Harris liked the one of herself with her two sons, David and James. We talked briefly, and I wondered if her sympathizers had sent the boxes of candy, cake, and fruit that sat on the table after they read about her hunger strike.

I visited Jean again when she was jailed at the Bedford Hills Correctional Facility, and it was strange to see the usually well-groomed woman wearing her hair white instead of red or blond. She also wore what appeared to be a waitress outfit. I assumed the dress was standard prison issue, but Harris had placed a fancy hem on it.

This time Harris wasn't as despondent and even told me she had made a magnificent friend in a well-educated woman who had produced plays on Broadway. I looked at Jean and said, "That could only be Adela Holtzer." Sure enough, it was the same woman I had covered when she was charged with fraud but poorly defended by Roy Cohn because she couldn't afford to pay him. Adela sat a short distance away, talking to her son. I'm glad I saw a happier Jean Harris during that last visit. Perhaps she had found a little peace of mind and come to grips with her mistakes.

THE ALMOST BACK-TO-BACK SHOOTINGS OF JOHN LENNON in December 1980 by Mark David Chapman and President Reagan in March 1981 by John W. Hinckley, Jr., crystallized my opinion of social misfits and started me thinking about how much better society would be without maintaining the lives of such sick people and without struggling to guarantee that they enjoyed the same legal options as the rest of us.

It was time to reassess, at least in my judgment, if laws applied to rational men could logically and realistically be applied to those so wounded by mental illness that they, in many respects, stopped functioning as human beings and became something other than our brothers and sisters. That was quite a step for me, since I had always, on principle, not approved the death penalty.

The acts of both Chapman and Hinckley spoke for themselves, and the public watched and read daily news about the details of each crime. In my role as a courtroom illustrator, I, too, took in all those dramatic developments and formulated my own vision of the assassins.

When Chapman was brought into the dingy arraignment hall in New York's Criminal Court, the first thing I noticed about him was his demonic looks. Chapman's brows knitted together in the middle of his face and then went winglike toward each side of his face. His eyes, blue but fringed with dark lashes—very similar to those of the "Son of Sam"—looked into space unknown to most people.

Chapman stood in front of the judge and simply stated that he was guilty of shooting John Lennon. Meanwhile, the prosecutor said it was a deliberate, premeditated act of murder, and Chapman's public defender said he was going to enter an insanity plea. The judge remanded Chapman to Bellevue Hospital and placed him on a suicide watch.

At his indictment, Chapman said he was mandated by God to plead guilty. Later the judge accepted a guilty plea to second-degree murder and then sentenced the man to a twenty-years-to-life term. During all of this, Chapman lost twenty pounds, and his attorney claimed that the "Son of Sam," who was incarcerated in the same hospital, had told his client that the food in the lockup was poisoned.

To make a pathetic situation even worse, Chapman's attorney later said that convicted killer Craig Crimmins had shaved Chapman's head. Kenneth Aronson, the attorney for Crimmins, admitted that his client might be "the Phantom of the Opera, but he was not the Barber of Seville."

The effect of these exchanges upon us in the courtroom resulted in an unofficial admission that these men weren't citizens of the same rank and class as the rest of us.

When I covered the arraignment of John W. Hinckley, Jr., in Washington, D.C., I thought in some ways it was an instant replay of the Chapman case. Hinckley, wearing a bulletproof vest under a navy blue sport jacket, sent a chill through me when I looked into his eyes. He appeared so wacked out, spaced out, and knocked out of the world around him. His reality wasn't one that we could even begin to understand.

Later, during one of the many hearings about the man's sanity, Hinckley seemed to drift into and out of consciousness. To me, Hinckley carried on a dialogue with himself. Every so often he smiled, looked serious, and then smiled again.

Defense attorney Vincent Fuller even stated that his client was driven by insane fantasies at the time of the Reagan assassination attempt. He introduced a lament that Hinckley wrote to singer John Lennon after Chapman had murdered him in 1980. In it, Hinckley wrote that heroes are meant to be killed, that guns are neat, that guns can kill extraordinary people with little effort, that the rich are getting richer, that Ronald Reagan never missed a beat and wasn't a fan of gun control, and that Western movies couldn't be made without guns.

After sitting through the Hinckley case and so many others involving misfits, I seriously thought that the legal, psychiatric, and religious communities should somehow find a way to deal better with the men and women who, because of mental illness, committed reprehensible acts of murder and torture.

If Hinckley, Chapman, Crimmins, Berkowitz, or other social misfits are ever permitted on the streets again, our society should seek retribution from those responsible for guaranteeing the safety of citizens because misfits live in another universe and play by rules known only to them. As demonstrated, they have killed or have injured innocent people on a whim or on a misbegotten "vision."

Quick Sketches

The life and death of Connie Crispwell, the daughter of a respected Virginia educator, brought anguish to all who sat through the trial of Robert Ransom. He was charged with strangling the woman after they had had intercourse and she had informed him that she was infected with AIDS. Her mother and sisters attended the trial, but they seemed so out of place in a New York City courtroom. The family, so aristocratic in appearance, were grim-faced as witnesses described what a "fun" person Connie had been and how much she enjoyed dancing the night away. Mrs. Crispwell concentrated, it seemed to me, on her knitting to escape the pain.

A woman district attorney worked hard for the guilty verdict, and she described the defendant as a black pimp and dope pusher who preyed on naïve young people. As the police detective brought in the trunk in which Crispwell's nude body had been found, the defendant looked indifferent. In all honesty, I had a difficult time sketching him. I wondered how many others he had murdered or had caused to die with his "business."

Ronald J. DeCasper stood motionless and speechless before Judge Seymour Rotker while being arraigned on a charge of stabbing a woman to death in a hospital. The defendant's eyes focused on something way out yonder in space, and he seemed totally oblivious to what was going on in court. But when the judge asked if arrangements had been made for a private defender, DeCasper changed his expression and said, "Yes, someone has been hired."

I had never seen anything quite like it before in court. It seemed as if the defendant opened the window to our world when he spoke to the judge and then quickly slammed it as he completed his answer. His eyes literally became glazed with a shiny but spooky transparent curtain. A few minutes later the prosecutor recounted how DeCasper went into the hospital room of a twenty-seven-year-old mother of four and stabbed her six times as she screamed, then bludgeoned her another ten times when she stopped screaming. A woman who shared the hospital room witnessed the attack and identified DeCasper.

* * *

The 1980 trial of Dr. John Buettner-Januschi, the author of the well-known book, *The Origins of Man,* provided a reminder that criminal ingenuity knows no economic or educational boundaries. The respected New York University anthropologist, who also had taught at Yale and Duke, was charged with making illegal drugs—LSD, methaqualone, synthetic cocaine—in his laboratory. He claimed that he made the drugs so he could use them in behavior modification studies on lemurs.

Throughout the trial, the anthropologist acted like he was above everyone else in intelligence and social status. But his imperial attitude backfired when the jury found the researcher guilty of making and selling illegal drugs and of lying to federal investigators.

Many of his friends cried that the conviction was part of a dirty politics campaign at the university. I didn't believe that for a second because I had sketched this unstable man in court. In 1987, Buettner-Januschi sent a box of Godiva chocolates to Charles Brient, Jr., the federal judge who sentenced him. Thinking it was a gift, the judge's wife took a bite and became ill. The diabolical professor had laced the chocolates with poison.

The arraignment of Alex J. Mengel in Westchester County for the slaying of a policeman brought yet another sinister man into court for crimes he might not even have comprehended. Mengel, a native of Guyana, appeared before the judge and looked and smelled as if he had been sleeping in dirty clothes in dark alleys near garbage dumpsters. His unevenly cut and unruly hair made him look like a wild man who had been scrounging the streets. It also was believed that Mengel had killed Beverly Capone, a programmer for International Business Machines Corporation who lived in Mount Vernon.

The woman had been missing since the death of the policeman, and Mengel used her car in his escape to Canada. Authorities there, before extraditing Mengel back to the United States, believed the defendant entered the country dressed as a woman. The scalp of a lady and skin from a human being were found in the car. Mengel, an amateur taxidermist, was suspected of using the dead woman's scalp as a wig when he entered Canada.

I admitted that when I heard that Mengel had been shot en route to the Westchester County Jail while trying to escape I felt justice had been served in this case. Even without a full trial, the evidence against this man seemed so overwhelming that it would have been a waste of taxpayer money and time to run Mengel through the judicial system. As I had painfully observed, the lives of some defendants weren't worth living.

THE ARRAIGNMENT AND TRIAL OF HAROLD WELLS AND MAX Lindenman were enough to make any rational person throw up. They were charged with raping, sodomizing, and brutally assaulting a Roman Catholic nun at the convent of the Sisters of Charity on East 116th Street in Manhattan. They even confessed to committing unspeakable atrocities on the nun, including carving twenty-seven crosses on the woman's body with a fingernail file.

This was a disgusting ordeal to sit through. Fortunately, there had been tremendous public feeling against these two men, and bail was denied. The judge even isolated the defendants on Riker Island for fear they would be attacked by other inmates.

IN 1979 I COVERED THE ARRAIGNMENT OF THREE MEN ACcused of robbery, burglary, possession of stolen property, and murder at a Brooklyn birthday party attended by fifty people. Charles Frankel, sixty-two, a professor at Columbia University and a former White House appointee, died after being shot three times in the head and the face and once in the chest by the men. His wife, a housekeeper, and an eighty-two-year-old woman also were murdered in the incident.

During the court proceedings, the defendants sat there with the biggest smiles on their faces. I couldn't believe that they were pleased and proud of being charged with such outlandish and criminal acts. Later one witness testified that the men had even showed him the gun they planned to use in the crime. But the one thing I never forgot about this trial was the moment when defendant Jimmie Lee Allen turned to me, smiled, and said, "Make me look like Robert Redford."

I HAD FINISHED SKETCHING A HEARING IN THE NEW YORK Criminal Court Building when I heard the booming voice of Judge Burton Roberts. "Ida," he said, "let's see what you did. Don't go yet. My next case is a young man who confessed to six murders." I thanked the judge, called the assignment desk with the news, and ended up being the only sketch artist in the city to capture the likeness of David Bullock, twenty-one, who admitted being a male prostitute and killing five men and one woman. A stocky black man dressed in what appeared to be designer jeans, Bullock gave a stunned Judge Roberts an exaggerated grin as he told him how "I enjoyed killing them. It was fun."

Roberts wasn't a man easily stunned. In his years as a judge, he had seen and heard it all in New York's "cesspool of humanity." This time, however, he turned and looked at me with a "Can you believe this?" look. Then Bullock described the killings in detail. He shot one victim to death while showing off a Christmas tree. The act of killing the man was so enjoyable that Bullock even wished the corpse "a Merry Christmas." Roberts didn't look amused, but Bullock laughed anyway.

"What's amusing about taking a man's life?" Roberts snapped. "It's fun," responded Bullock. Then he related how he took credit cards from his victims, but the murderer said he never stole their clothes because "it's bad luck to wear a dead man's clothes." He also left their jewelry since "I'm not into it."

After the mass murderer described the death of each victim, Judge Roberts tried to take the smile off the cocky killer's face by sentencing him to 150 years in prison before he'd be eligible for parole. The case ended a killing spree that spanned forty days, and Roberts let loose and verbally pounded this ". . . angel of death. You will stay in jail for the rest of your life. You became a monster and a viper. When you die, you will go to a higher court—a Supreme Being. I don't know what will happen to you there."

District Attorney Pat Dugan also added his feelings on the case. "As a child," the prosecutor said, "David Bullock enjoyed watching animals die. If he is allowed to walk the streets, he will kill again."

SEVEN

Outcasts and Traitors

THE SINGLE MOST VIVID IMPRESSION I HAD OF OUTCASTS and traitors whom I sketched in court was that they all seemed to be such opportunists. They were people without any conscience, and they sold themselves to the highest bidder. They didn't care how many people were killed or how many people were injured as long as they achieved their sadistic goal or secret mission. Stepping on dead bodies was often the intent rather than the means by which they became successful in crimes against humanity or in crimes against another sovereign nation.

We've all read about war criminals and traitors who got away with their crimes, but some were caught and stood trial. When they found themselves before a judge in a U.S. courtroom, they universally said, "No, it was not me. I didn't do those things."

Watching and sketching at these cases provided some of the saddest memories of my career. In the face of often overwhelming testimony to the contrary, these people cowardly denied their deeds and then, especially accused Nazi war criminals, somehow found the financial resources and government clout to drag out legal proceedings for years.

My first exposure to an outcast, Hermine Braunsteiner Ryan, a Queens woman accused of committing war crimes, occurred in 1973 during a preliminary hearing held on the fourteenth floor of the U.S. Immigration and Naturalization Service's New York headquarters, across from the federal courthouse on Foley Square. Pat Collins, my reporter, pointed to a couple and said, "That's the housewife who reportedly was a guard and supervisor at Ravensbrück and Lublin Majdanek concentration camps in Poland, and her husband, Russell Ryan, an American."

I stared at a woman, who looked like a witch with short, blond hair, bangs, and a long, sharp nose that curved down to meet a sharp chin. In between the nose and chin, a thin mouth curved downward. Through thin slits, I barely determined that the woman had blue eyes. A chill went through me. I had read about men accused of atrocities, but this was the first woman I ever recalled being brought into court and confronted with charges of committing crimes against humanity.

The judged ruled that Ryan may have entered the country under false pretenses and sent the case to trial in federal court in Brooklyn. West Germany had already requested that the United States extradite the woman to face charges of committing four murders and of assisting with one thousand other killings.

In court, we listened to the testimony of witnesses' horrible memories, including the unprovoked whipping death of a woman inmate and the hanging of a fourteen-year-old girl in which Hermine Braunsteiner placed a stool under the girl because she was short. The witness also testified that before the noose was tightened around the girl's neck, she stared at the other inmates and said, "Remember me."

I tried to sketch and not to listen to that kind of testimony. It was, however, impossible to avoid the pain that went with comprehending what Braunsteiner did as a guard in concentration camps. Throughout the testimony, a smirk flashed across Hermine's face. To me, that woman was a brutal monster.

I also wondered how a Queens housewife could afford high-priced attorney John J. Barry, and a reporter volunteered the answer. He had heard about a secret organization that dedicated itself to the protection of Nazis who stood trial. The network used the acronym Odessa, which stood for the formal German title *Organisation der Ehemaligen SS Angehorigen.* But the money didn't help Hermine Braunsteiner Ryan; she lost the extradition proceeding and eventually found herself on trial in West Germany.

Another extradition case of an accused Nazi war criminal took place a few years later when the Immigration and Naturalization Service reviewed the circumstances of how Boleslavs Maikovskis, a Latvian émigré, entered the United States after World War II.

When I first saw him, in 1977, Maikovskis looked quite dapper in a blue suit, pale blue shirt, and blue and red tie. He sat quietly with his hands folded and showed no emotion whatsoever as U.S. District Attorney James W. Grable told the court about the statements he had obtained from witnesses who stated Maikovskis had inspired, organized, and led the massacre of inhabitants in the village of Audrini, Latvia.

The federal attorney described how German soldiers, with the help of Maikovskis, the chief of the 2nd Police District in Rēzekne, stormed into the village and Latvian police aided the soldiers in rousting people out of their houses into the street.

One witness told Grable that Maikovskis had ridden erect on a Thoroughbred trotting horse stolen from a farmer as he led a column of prisoners—men, women, and children—out of the village, which was engulfed in flames. Women were separated from men, and the men were taken to the jail in Rēzekne.

The method used to kill the prisoners was sadistically efficient. The men were taken into the marketplace ten at a time and placed in two rows, with one group kneeling in front of the group standing. The shots fired into the heads of those kneeling passed through, then into the stomachs of those standing.

We discovered that Maikovskis had been awarded the German Order of Merit and the German Cross for his actions, but the man's glory didn't last long because Soviet forces advancing on the Eastern Front eventually took control of the area and Maikovskis fled to Germany.

After swearing that he never advocated or assisted in the persecution of any person because of race, religion, or national origin, the former police chief obtained residency status in 1948 as a displaced person and settled in Brooklyn. He worked as a carpenter and became active in Latvian cultural anti-communist groups. Like hundreds of thousands of American servicemen who returned home after the war, Maikovskis saved his money and fulfilled the American dream of buying a house. He lived in Mineola, New York, where he was cordial with neighbors but didn't make any real friends.

His role in the village massacre had been publicly disclosed in 1965 during a Latvian trial when surviving eyewitnesses described the carnage and testified that Maikovskis directed and participated in the killing. The court found the former police chief guilty of war crimes, and the Latvian S.S.R. asked the United States for his extradition.

Our government reportedly refused the request because it didn't recognize Latvia as part of the Soviet Union. Fortunately, the Immigration and Naturalization Service pursued its own investigation to see if Maikovskis had lied about his background when he entered the United States. If so, he could be deported.

That was when the case began to get controversial because several agencies of our own government seemed to be at odds over the proceedings. But nothing seemed to daunt the former police chief, and he always seemed to have enough money to afford top legal advisers, even when the evidence piled up against him and the outcome looked gloomy. A professor from Germany as well as two women who had been inmates in a Nazi concentration camp testified about his activities.

However, it also was discovered that Maikovskis had been vice chairman of a mysterious and well-financed Washington, D.C.-based organization called the American Latvian Association and had served as a delegate to the European Assembly of Captive Nations. That bizarre twist in the case later made a great deal of sense when we learned that the Assembly had been a front organization for one of our intelligence agencies, and Maikovskis undoubtedly had been an anti-Soviet agent secretly brought to this country after the outbreak of the Cold War. In the end, though, the preponderance of evidence against Boleslavs Maikovskis resulted in his extradition to the Soviet Union.

Much of what I experienced in the Maikovskis extradition hearings prepared me for the Karl Linnas case. He was accused of being a Nazi officer in a concentration camp in Estonia where twelve thousand people were executed, and the case began in 1981 and ended in 1985 after his attorneys took the case to the U.S. Court of Appeals and to the U.S. Supreme Court. Linnas himself frequently didn't show up to hear the horrifying testimony that he was responsible for tens of thousands of deaths. It was truly hard to imagine that those crimes could go unpunished for so long in a civilized society, but the United States finally extradited Linnas to the Soviet Union; he faced the survivors of his brutality, but unfortunately Linnas died of recurring health problems before the Soviet legal system completed the trial. It was a pity that he passed away before the Soviet authorities had a chance to hand out their brand of justice to this Nazi war criminal.

In 1978 I covered the espionage trial of two Soviet citizens, Valdik A. Enger and Rudolf P. Chernyayev, who worked at the United Nations but tried to obtain sensitive information about a U.S. Navy underwater warfare project. They had been arrested on the New Jersey Garden State Parkway, which served as one of their "drop-offs," with U.S. government documents in their possession. Another man, a Soviet diplomat who had been with Enger and Chernyayev, was arrested but released because of the immunity given to the diplomatic corps.

Enger and Chernyayev looked like the Soviet version of Abbott and Costello. Fat and unattractive, Enger spoke English quite well and appeared to be the boss of the spy team. Chernyayev wore Savile Row clothes and pretended he didn't speak English.

No one questioned the outcome of this trial. A U.S. naval officer, who had been given twenty thousand dollars to supply the Soviets with bogus "secret" documents, testified at the trial, and the duo was found guilty and sentenced to fifty years each in federal prison.

At one point during the trial, Enger turned to me and smirkingly said, "You know, I did not do a thing. This is all political. They are just doing this to harass me."

Because of the ever-complicated chess game combining espionage and politics between the United States and the Soviet Union, I thought that these men would never serve a day in prison—and they didn't. While appealing their convictions, they were released in the custody of Soviet ambassador Anatoli F. Dobrynin. A prisoner exchange was later arranged, with Enger and Chernyayev given back to the Soviets for an American businessman and five refuseniks.

The U.S. district attorney who handled the case called me after the exchange had been made and said that Enger had been as cavalier as ever at his departure. "I am sorry that we had to meet under these conditions," Enger said as he shook the attorney's hand. "I would have enjoyed meeting you under different circumstances." Then the healthy and chubby spy walked away. On the other hand, the district attorney claimed that the released American, who was weak and thin, looked as if he had been tortured in a Soviet gulag.

I returned to the courtroom in 1983 to see another proceeding involving the United States and the Soviet Union. This time, though, the issue was both trivial and comical. A Cold War had erupted between the community of Glen Cove, New York, and Soviet diplomats and their families. The Soviets, who occupied posh estates on Long Island Sound, wanted to use the local beaches, tennis courts, and golf courses free of charge because of their diplomatic status. The Long Island community, however, claimed that the Soviets were not entitled to use the facilities because they didn't pay any property taxes.

In reality, Glen Cove lost an estimated one hundred thousand dollars in revenues yearly because it couldn't legally collect property taxes on the Soviet estates. As incredible as it may seem, the State Department sided with the Soviets and spent fifteen months trying to work out an agreement between Glen Cove and the diplomats.

When Glen Cove mayor Allen Parente proposed that the Soviets use the facilities for a yearly user's fee of six hundred dollars in lieu of taxes, the situation escalated into a major legal battle. The Justice Department then filed a suit to force Glen Cove into opening its recreational facilities free to the Soviets and gave the town twenty days to prepare its defense.

The mayor even appeared in court and testified that he couldn't guarantee the safety of Soviet diplomats in the wake of the downing of the Korean Air Lines jumbo jet over Soviet airspace. Fortunately, cool heads prevailed and Glen Cove went back to the bargaining table with the Soviets, the Justice Department, and the State Department. After three months of skillful diplomacy, Glen Cove lifted its two-year ban on the use of recreational facilities and allowed the Russians onto its beaches and into its locker rooms.

The chess game between the Americans and the Soviets took an interesting twist in 1986 when Soviet physicist Gennadi F. Zakharov, assigned to the U.N. Secretariat, was arrested on a Queens subway platform as he gave one thousand dollars to an American defense contractor for three classified documents.

Zakharov, who had been an officer in the KGB, had earlier sought the help of a Guyanese student. A permanent resident alien in the United States, the student contacted the FBI. Zakharov had been trying to obtain classified information on a jet engine design. Because he didn't hold diplomatic status, he faced a life sentence in a federal prison if convicted.

I met Zakharov during his arraignment in Brooklyn before Magistrate Carol Amon, who denied a request that the Soviet be released on bail and another that he be released in the custody of the Soviet ambassador. Zakharov, who looked more like a dapper businessman than a spy, thus became the center of an international controversy.

In retaliation for his arrest, the Soviets hauled in *U.S. News & World Report* Moscow correspondent Nicholas Daniloff and accused him of spying for the United States. In the middle of all this, I happened to be in the federal courthouse in Brooklyn, where the FBI's informant in the Zakharov case was testifying before a grand jury. I walked right past the Guyanese student, turned around to get another look at him, went right to my portfolio, and did a sketch of the student from memory.

After a deal in which Zakharov was to be traded for Daniloff had been worked out in Moscow and Washington, I sketched Zakharov one last time in federal court. At the end of the proceeding, Zakharov marched out with his attorney, turned to me, and gave me a big smile followed by a condescending wink, as if he knew all along he was going to win the chess game. I don't know if Soviet spies are trained to expect that somehow or in some way they will be released if caught on a mission in the

United States, but that sure was the way it worked out most of the time.

One of the most exciting assignments I ever undertook for NBC News was the re-creation of the infamous Sacco-Vanzetti trial, which was held in 1921 in Dedham, Massachusetts. Ever since my college days, I had believed that this trial represented one of the greatest miscarriages of justice in this century. It smacked of racism and political persecution, and the trial certainly didn't represent the ideals embedded in the Constitution nor the principles of Anglo-American law.

I was given the assignment in 1977 by Richard Hunt, the talented producer who worked with the New York bureau of NBC News. He pegged the story to the upcoming posthumous pardon Massachusetts Governor Michael Dukakis was to give Sacco, and Hunt wanted viewers to relive the trial through the use of my sketches.

Hunt had spent a great deal of time researching the case and made what could have been a tedious assignment for me into an experience of a lifetime. After personally briefing me on the case and what he hoped to see on my sketchpad, I flew to Boston, where two members of the NBC bureau had arranged that I confer with a friend of theirs who worked at the local library and who happened to be an authority on the trial.

From there I drove to Dedham and visited the original courtroom where Nicola Sacco and Bartolomeo Vanzetti were tried and convicted for the robbery of a shoe factory payroll of slightly more than fifteen thousand dollars and for the murder of Frederick A. Parmenter and Alessandro Berrardelli in the nearby town of South Braintree. I sketched the cage in which Sacco and Vanzetti—and every defendant—had been placed in those days; for whatever reason, it had been stored in the courthouse basement.

Then I spent considerable time sitting in the courtroom and absorbing the scene because it was so different in appearance from what I had been accustomed to seeing in New York and New Jersey. Little, if anything, had been changed in the courtroom appearance since the days of the Sacco-Vanzetti trial. The judge's bench, made of walnut and adorned with beautiful carvings, impressed me. The judge sat in a large leather chair, and behind him stood a bookcase filled with law books, which I had never before seen in a courtroom. I guessed that the judge could easily reach for the right book in case he needed to check a legal point or a particular statute. An old-fashioned round clock with a pendulum hung above the bookcase.

The clerk's bench was situated right in front of the judge's bench, the jury box to the left, and the witness stand adjacent to the jury box. I had seen a similar witness stand during the divorce proceeding of Senator Edward Brooke; it was a circular shelf held up by poles, and the witness stood rather than sat through testimony and cross-examination. The defendants' cage, it was pointed out to me, stood in the center of the room in front of the spectators. Although it held people captive, the cage, constructed of thin metal strips, allowed the defendant to view the proceedings easily. Amusingly enough, a metal decoration adorned the top of the cage.

After I sketched the courtroom scene, I drove back to Boston, and our expert on the trial sat me in front of a microfilm monitor in the library. I carefully read the *Boston Globe*'s daily account of the six-week trial. This research proved crucial for the television re-creation and insightful for me in terms of how the judicial system operated in a less tolerant America.

In the 1920s, a great deal of anti-Italian sentiment had erupted in Boston. I sincerely thought that was one reason why Sacco and Vanzetti did so poorly in the trial. The foreman of the jury even stated before the trial officially began that the men should get what was coming to them whether they committed the crime or not. The judge had once even pointed out to the jury that the defendants had been in the United States for eleven years and still couldn't speak English.

Vanzetti didn't help his case, though, when he testified that he was a bachelor, a fish peddler, and an anarchist. In those post-World War I days, Americans were resentful of anyone who didn't believe in democracy, especially anarchists and Communists. It also was rumored that the judge, Webster Thayer, had even made derogatory comments about the defendants, calling them "anarchist bastards."

Although history has made Sacco a less articulate figure than Vanzetti, Sacco vehemently denied his participation in the robbery-murder. He testified that he had worked at the shoe factory for seven years and was absent only one time, the day of the crime; that the hat found at the crime scene wasn't his, and he even tried it on to show the hat was too small; that he was forced to pose for witnesses and was not identified in a lineup but rather in jail.

It also was demonstrated in court that the gun barrel of Sacco's .32-caliber Colt automatic could easily have been switched with the barrel of another pistol and may not have been the weapon used in the crime. Witnesses in the case changed their stories, and the defense attorney (who was a member of the controversial Labor Party and had never tried a criminal case) and the prosecutor both doctored evidence to support their cases.

How the judge allowed the case to continue let alone permit the jury to render a verdict was beyond me. From what I read in newspaper stories, the judge had more than enough reason to declare a mistrial. But even if a mistrial had not been declared, a competent attorney should have been able to find grounds for a successful appeal of the conviction.

Although their execution had been delayed from 1921 until 1927, Sacco and Vanzetti underwent what I considered one of the worst injustices of modern American history. They didn't receive a fair trial and were convicted, in my judgment, because of their ethnic background and because of their political beliefs. In this case, Sacco and Vanzetti were judged as outcasts and paid for the crime with their lives.

Quick Sketches

When authorities brought former Central Intelligence Agency employee Edwin P. Wilson into Brooklyn's federal courthouse for arraignment on illegally selling arms to Libya, he looked exhausted and as angry as any defendant I've ever seen. Justice Department agents had set up an elaborate trap that lured the renegade arms dealer from the Dominican Republic to New York's Kennedy International Airport, where he was arrested.

Wilson, a wheeler-dealer who had avoided law enforcement authorities for years and still managed to do business with the likes of Colonel Muammar Qaddafi, reminded me of an Atlantic City gambler who believed he could beat all the odds and break the casino but instead lost his house, life savings, and car in one roll of the dice at the craps table.

EIGHT

Stranger Than Fiction

IN FIFTEEN YEARS OF SKETCHING IN THE COURTROOM, I NEVER knew what to expect. One case would make me laugh, and another would make me cry. So often, though, I was utterly surprised by the bizarre crimes defendants were accused of perpetrating or by the strange circumstances surrounding cases. I've never met a fiction writer capable of dreaming up some of the wacky things I've witnessed during trials.

One of the most bizarre cases and assignments I ever undertook for NBC occurred in February 1979. My phone rang, and it was the network overseas desk. "Ida, would you be available for an assignment in Guyana?" the editor asked. Of course, I knew this was a very special and perhaps a very dangerous assignment, and I discussed it with my husband before accepting.

Two NBC employees I personally knew, Bob Harris and Bob Brown, had been killed with Congressman Leo J. Ryan at Port Kaituma Airport in the jungle near Jonestown, Guyana, during an investigation of the People's Temple run by maniacal Jim Jones. Shortly after the murders, cult leader Jones convinced 911 of his followers to commit suicide by drinking Kool-Aid laced with cyanide. The Guyanese government had already arrested a man named Larry Layton, a lieutenant under Jones, and charged him with the murder of four people at the airport. NBC didn't let the story fade away and had a personal motive for wanting to cover the trial and for seeing that justice was served.

Later, when I called the network graphics department, I also learned that the assignment was going to be a technically challenging one, too. "Ida," said Lee Stausland, the head of graphics, "stop by the office before you leave for Guyana, and I'll give you some special research material. You know, of course, that you won't be able to sketch in court. Everything will have to be done from your memory. Knowing you've done a trial before that way, I hope you won't have too much to copy."

Lee's package was a big help, and I tucked the material into my art portfolio with my sketchpad the night before I was to leave. My husband, Ed, seemed quite concerned about me taking this assignment. "Remember, two of your fellow employees have been killed down there already," he warned. "So don't go anywhere without your reporter and film crew. Guyana isn't a place for sightseeing."

Just before we fell asleep, the NBC travel department called and said a small package would be delivered to me at the airport fifteen minutes before I boarded my plane the next day. I couldn't imagine what it would be, but I said okay anyway.

As passengers boarded the flight to Guyana, my package hadn't yet arrived at Kennedy International Airport. So I raced to a telephone and called the travel department. They put me on hold while they did a radio check of the delivery. "It's coming through the door at this very moment!" the dispatcher yelled. Well, my delivery wasn't a small package at all. It was a crate that contained twenty-four gallons of Deer Park water. I guessed that the NBC brass didn't trust the quality of the drinking water in Guyana and didn't trust government officials who might have been in cahoots with Jim Jones and wanted to further discourage NBC News from fully covering the trial by tampering with our water supply.

I didn't know what to do with the crate. As tears began streaming down my face, a man working for the airline passed by, and I related how two of our employees had already been killed in Guyana and how important the water was to my own safety. "Don't worry," he said, "we'll get the container on the plane." With that, I pulled out a twenty-dollar bill and gave it to him. A few seconds later another airline employee came by and effortlessly moved my container of water to the plane. I also gave him a twenty-dollar bill and felt better about having safe water to drink in an unfriendly country.

After arriving in Guyana, the first words out of the producer's mouth were, "Did you bring the water?" He was so relieved to know it had arrived with me. The chauffeur who drove us from the airport to the hotel was the same man who escorted Brown, Harris, and Ryan on their trip. That unnerved me, and I felt a chill. The reality of the assignment finally settled into my mind and into my nerves.

The next morning I learned that Bob Hager, whom I had worked with so many times before, was the reporter for my story. He knew me well and immediately asked if I wanted to sneak a look at the courtroom after breakfast or lunch. When we arrived at the deserted courthouse, I was surprised to find it an English Gothic structure similar to the buildings near my home on the Jersey Shore. We went inside the building and took photographs. Then I sat down and began to sketch the interior of the room because I knew I would be prohibited from doing any of that during the actual proceeding. Bob watched every stroke I made on the sketchpad.

But suddenly we were surrounded by armed Guyanese guards and policemen. I held on to Bob as the men grabbed my Polaroid camera, pulled the film out, and confiscated my sketch. They marched us down to the police station, but I managed to slip several of the exposed and developed pictures from the Polaroid to Hager. When we informed the chief of police that we worked for NBC News, he seemed quite sympathetic but also informed us that it was illegal to take pictures of the court, even when it wasn't in session.

Although the chief released us, I was confused and frightened. However, the authorities couldn't keep me from sketching in my hotel room, and I pulled out my supplies and re-created the courtroom in a sketch from memory. That pleased me. Not only was I prepared for the trial to begin, but also sketching relieved the tension that had built up inside me from our encounter with armed guards.

It seemed as if all the world's reporters, cameramen, and illustrators descended on Georgetown the next day. We were ushered en masse into the courtroom and seated on wooden benches. Larry Layton, a skeletal-looking man, sat in a docket British-style. The docket itself was surrounded by soldiers. The attorneys wore robes, and the judge was seated on a very high bench. Like many parts of the Caribbean and Central America, Guyana was comprised of a mixture of races. Looking at the people in the courtroom, I couldn't help thinking that British colonials had first brought Africans to this country, followed by East Indians and Orientals. I took careful notes but didn't sketch anything whatsoever.

After the session, I raced to the car and sketched as fast as I could. We drove back to the hotel, where my work was taped and then transmitted to the United States via satellite. After dinner, Hager handed me a local newspaper with a headline that read, "Two U.S. Reporters Interrogated."

Hager also said that my sketches had "looked very good

on the air" for NBC, and we wrapped up a successful trip. I captured the courtroom scene during Layton's trial, and Bob captured a forty-five-minute tape of the mass poisoning in Jonestown. The tape was found near a wooden chair that served as cult leader Jim Jones' throne during his reign of terror in Guyana.

ONE THING I NEVER THOUGHT WOULD HAPPEN TO ME IN MY job with NBC was to become familiar with cults. I ended up covering parents who kidnapped their children to secure their safe return from every imaginable religious or fanatic organization, including the Rastafarians in Philadelphia, the Church of Satan, the Church of Scientology, the Hare Krishnas, the followers of Ethiopian emperor Haile Selassie, and the Unification Church.

The most well-known group, the Unification Church, was founded by the Reverend Sun Myung Moon. His Moonies numbered three million, and he had a firm hold over his worshipers. I also covered the controversial leader twice in 1982 during two important court cases in which he testified. In fact, Moon had been charged in the first case with using phony ledgers and documents to cheat the government out of one hundred sixty-two thousand dollars in federal taxes. He sat quietly with his eyes closed, as if he put himself in a trance and tried to block out the testimony given against him. It seemed to me that there wasn't much anyone could do for him because the prosecution had a solid case. Moon was convicted of tax evasion, but he didn't bat an eye. One of his supporters, though, did carry on about the injustice of the case.

Dr. Mose Durst believed the court had been bamboozled by government prosecutors because they repeated the word "cash" over and over again until the jury was brainwashed. That amused me. After all, I had heard about cult brainwashing, even among the Moonies. I was surprised that the man even brought up the issue.

Durst said that the only way to get to Moon was to do it through the Internal Revenue Service. He also said that Moon, like all the world's great religious leaders, had been subjected to hatred, bigotry, and misunderstanding. That was one man's opinion.

Believe it or not, Moon testified in federal court the week after his own conviction. He had hoped to assist one of his followers, Anthony Colombrito, in winning a nine-million-dollar damage suit against deprogrammer Galen Kelly, but ended up destroying the case and part of his own reputation.

While on the witness stand, Moon testified that he had met Jesus, Moses, and Buddha. He said that all of them had identified themselves to him in Korean. Moon also claimed that he, the leader of the Unification Church, may very well become the true Messiah, the reincarnation of Jesus. In fact, during one of the revelations Jesus even asked Moon to help him with the salvation of the universe.

I had a hard time concentrating on my sketches while all this wild testimony was going on. Although Moon used an interpreter to translate his answers from Korean into English, I was surprised that Moon made such incredible statements. If he hadn't already hurt the damage suit enough, Moon also told the court that he lived in a six-hundred-twenty-five-thousand-dollar estate with his second wife and twelve children. The information supported the contention of many people that this man was another religious imposter in the business to make money and nothing more.

Although many of his followers sat in court with a dazed sort of obedience, the suit was halted by a federal appeals court motion. But Colombrito admitted he initiated the motion and withdrew the case because his worst fears about a trial concerning the Unification Church had been realized, and he wanted to save Moon from further public suffering. He said the government had turned the trial into an inquisition with the only purpose being to discredit the church and to ridicule Moon.

The leader of Colombrito's own church managed to do that all by himself, but perhaps a brainwashed cult follower couldn't understand the reality of the situation. Later I was elated when I learned that I had again been nominated for another Emmy Award for my work during this leader's tax evasion trial.

WHEN JOHNSON & JOHNSON PHARMACEUTICAL MOGUL J. Seward Johnson died, he should have stipulated in his will that corporate officials place a Band-Aid over the mouth of each of his six grown children. My God, they hung the family dirty laundry out to dry in 1986 for everyone to see when they contested the will and challenged an award of over half a billion dollars to his third wife, Barbara "Basia" Piasecaa Johnson. Although she didn't testify during the proceedings, Basia took a public-relations pounding from the children. They alleged all sorts of things: that their father was senile, that Basia exerted undue influence on him to change his will thirty-nine days before he died, that Seward kept a gun near his bed to protect himself from Basia.

But it was the oldest child, Mary Lea Johnson, who ripped apart Basia in the battle for the big bucks. On the stand Mary Lea showed a large, blown-up aerial view of the palatial home that Seward had built for his third wife. It was implied that Basia, a Polish immigrant who spoke only a few words of English when she started to work as a chambermaid at the Johnson estate some twelve years earlier, didn't love Seward and only wanted his money.

After divorcing his wife of thirty-two years, Seward married Basia and began work on a palace he call Jasna Polana, after Tolstoy's estate. Basia supervised the construction of the place during a four-year period, and reportedly she made it into one of the most elegant homes in the country. Priceless Greek and Roman antiquities filled the house. The estate contained a seventy-two-foot swimming pool, marble bathtubs with jacuzzi and gold-plated towel racks, an orchard house, and an air-conditioned doghouse.

When Johnson was invested in the Knights of Columbus, Basia reportedly spent a quarter million dollars on china embossed with the Maltese cross, and another ninety thousand dollars for crystal.

During the seventeen-week proceedings thirty-three witnesses testified about Seward's marriage to Basia. It was sad for me to sit through the testimony because I felt like an intruder in a family argument. I was truly embarrassed to hear about the private life of this couple.

In the end, the case never went to the jury. I remember meeting Judge Marie Lambert in the courthouse lobby the day a settlement was to be announced. She told me that she had been up all night working out the details of the agreement with the heirs. I sat in the front row of the courtroom when the judge stated that Basia had agreed to pay one hundred sixty million dollars to the six Johnson children, which left her with three hundred fifty million.

Since each Johnson heir was already a multimillionaire based on other awards from Seward, I wondered why, with all the money they already had, they allowed their family's private and financial affairs to become public information. I always thought that people with a great deal of money liked to keep their privacy. In this case, however, it seemed greed overruled reason.

ONE OF THE MOST BIZARRE CASES I EVER COVERED WENT TO trial in 1986 but actually began in 1979, when Bobby McLaughlin was wrongly accused and convicted of murder and robbery in Brooklyn Marine Park. McLaughlin had been identified by a lone witness as one of three men who robbed fifteen to twenty children in the park and then murdered nineteen-year-old Robert Halstad. Robert Tovin, then fifteen, said McLaughlin was the killer.

McLaughlin received a fifteen-years-to-life sentence for the crime.

For six years, McLaughlin protested his conviction, and a civil liberties lawyer took up his cause. When the case was reopened, everyone learned that Tovin's identification had been made under "suggestive tactics" by the police. I took great pride in covering the 1986 hearings into the murder because WNBC's John Miller always had been convinced of McLaughlin's innocence and did many stories on the case. Other reporters looked at the case and pursued the story.

The foreman of the jury stated on a television program that if the jury that convicted McLaughlin had known then what he knew now, they never would have rendered a guilty verdict.

Judge Ann Feldman reviewed the case and ruled that McLaughlin didn't commit the crime. She even said that she wanted to free him that very moment, but release procedures would last about an hour. McLaughlin's foster father jumped over the front row of seats and grabbed his son in a bear hug. It truly was a beautiful scene, and I captured it on my sketchpad.

And when Bobby McLaughlin walked out of the courthouse, he knelt down on the stairs and seemed to kiss the ground. He was so thrilled to be free again, but I don't know if he was aware that the day of his release was July Fourth.

Quick Sketches

The trial of Lester Zygmaniak, charged with the 1973 slaying of his brother George, was a difficult case for me. All of us in the courtroom endured the sad circumstances surrounding the case. Lester, twenty-three, finally gave in to his brother's repeated requests to kill him after a motorcycle accident had left George paralyzed from the neck down. In fact, George begged Lester to put him out of his misery. Finally Lester shot him, but George fell into a coma and remained unconscious until his death.

Since the trial took place in Freehold, New Jersey, where a state canon prohibited all photographs and sketches of any courtroom proceeding, I took notes and dashed outside to do fast re-creations. It was the first time I had been required to work from memory, and I also did sketches of George from photographs I saw of him. Robert Ansell, the defense attorney, did a fine job of dealing with all the complex legal, ethical, and medical aspects involved in a case of mercy killing. He said that Lester had been so pained by his brother's condition and repeated demands to die that the defendant had become temporarily insane.

After Lester testified, I thought the insanity plea had been a good idea. It provided an out for the jury. Ansell, who earlier had wanted the charge dismissed because he believed that no crime was committed because George had consented to his own death, worked hard to establish the love and the bond that had been established by the brothers. In the end, the jury decided that Lester's actions were based on love as well as on a temporary lapse into insanity, and acquitted him.

WILLIAM BOSKET, JR., WAS SENTENCED TO ONLY FIVE YEARS in jail for an eight-day crime spree in New York City that included the killing of two subway riders. His 1978 trial resulted in a change in state law that permitted any juvenile who committed murder to be tried as an adult. Not long after he began serving his five years, Bosket was found guilty of attempted murder in the stabbing of a prison guard at Shawangunk Correctional Facility in Wallkill, New York.

For that and other crimes, he was sentenced to a minimum of fifteen years to life in prison. Bosket later stated that his only regret was that he didn't kill the guard and that the New York legal system had made him a monster. I almost threw up when I heard that. Bosket, like so many misfits, blamed somebody else for his evil actions. It always was someone else's fault. But there was no question in anyone's mind that Bosket was a monster, a self-created monster.

STILL ANOTHER CASE NOT TO BE BELIEVED CONCERNED Margaret Turner, the so-called Borgia Prostitute. She ran a slick operation out of the Vista Hotel in the World Trade Center in which she served "johns" cocktails laced with various substances that rendered them immobile. After the men were unconscious, their possessions were stolen from the hotel. The scheme was uncovered when a bank official from Buffalo, New York, was found dead in the hotel of scopolamine poisoning.

For some reason, Turner had a passion for blond hair, and that was her undoing, because witnesses came forward with testimony that they had seen the man with a blonde. I thought that Turner, a black woman in her fifties, looked rather ridiculous in court because the platinum in her hair had worn thin and it was obvious that she needed to have her hair set again because it looked like it had been swept by a vacuum cleaner.

IN 1984 I COVERED A COURT SQUABBLE INVOLVING SEVERAL Jewish groups. The Lubovitchers, a Hasidic sect, brought the Satmars, an Orthodox group, to court on beard-cutting charges. That's right, beard-cutting charges. But by the time the two groups met again in court, the beards had grown back. But the Jewish men were quite upset about my being in court sketching them.

According to their beliefs, a woman's place was in the

home, where she kept her hair short and wore a *sheitle*—a wig. They didn't believe in women working. The fact was that every time one of the men looked at me he put his hand over his face, as if to blot out my image. The judge, Neil Firetog, showed great patience and listened to the complaints of these men quite sympathetically.

CIBELLA BORGES, TWENTY-FIVE, TESTIFIED ON HER OWN BEHALF in 1982 during a New York Police Department hearing after she had been suspended without pay from her position as a vice squad cop. She was relieved of her duties following publication of a magazine picture spread that showed Borges in the buff. Pleading not guilty to unprofessional conduct, Borges claimed she had posed for the magazine before she became a cop.

However, she admitted to being "sweet-talked" into the compromising pictorial by the photographer. Borges said that she had undergone ovarian surgery and had been on a "self-destruction trip" when she encountered the photographer. He told her she had a beautiful body and would be perfect for modeling. Borges told the police panel she also "felt attractive and like a real woman" when she talked to the man. He even convinced her that no one would ever recognize her in the photos.

Well, I was totally astonished that the woman had doubts about her own sexuality and even more taken aback by what I thought was sexual harassment and chauvinistic behavior of male police officials. After all, how many male officers had posed for muscle magazines or similar publications?

IN MY ESTIMATION, THE JUDICIAL SYSTEM PRODUCED A precedent-setting case of sorts in 1979 when Virginia O'Hare brought suit against Dr. Howard Belin for positioning her belly button off-center after tummy tuck surgery. O'Hare, who had already subjected herself to a nose job and an eye-lift, claimed that a centered belly button was a valuable feminine attribute.

The jury agreed and awarded the woman eight hundred fifty-four thousand dollars in damages. Dr. Belin called the verdict ridiculous. "They awarded," he decried, "a healthy woman with two arms, two legs, and both of her eyes an enormous sum of money. What are they going to give someone who was really injured?"

NINE

Lawyers and Judges

MY FIRST EXPERIENCE WATCHING AND SKETCHING ATTORNEYS as a television courtroom illustrator turned out to be an awful artistic disappointment. After studying prints of the great French artist Honoré Daumier, I secretly expected to see attorneys gesturing in long, black robes. I immediately discovered that only judges wore robes and only a few courtrooms had the feeling of regal elegance as depicted in Daumier's work.

Lawyers wore business suits; some looked quite dapper in expensive tailored pinstripes, while other attorneys appeared to have literally slept in inexpensive and worn suits. The lawyers moved, gestured, and provoked responses from the judge, witnesses, and the opposing attorney. In reality, they directed the "show" in the courtroom, and depending on the personality of the defense attorney, the "show" would be exciting or dull.

I could sense if the attorney was properly prepared for the case or if the attorney had great interest in the client by body movement and the opening statement. Some lawyers lit up the court with their energy and electricity from the moment they entered the courtroom.

It seemed that most lawyers fit into one of four categories: actor, politician, libertarian, or pedant. But no matter what kind of courtroom persona, lawyers always played the most important roles in any trial. Attorneys also wrote the scripts for client testimony, choreographed maneuvers around the strategy of the opposing attorney, and sometimes rewrote the material to play on the sentiments of the jury during closing arguments.

Lawyers knew how to protect their clients and simultaneously how to handle witnesses. Many virtually cast a hypnotic spell over the witnesses, jury, and courtroom gallery. They repeated what they wanted the jury to hear from the witness over and over again until somehow the witness would actually repeat it. I found the examination and cross-examination of witnesses absolutely fascinating.

If attorneys played the role of directors in the courtroom, then judges acted as producers, and everyone knew that they controlled the stage. Most judges were gracious, but they catered to the jury and the public and what they should or shouldn't hear. Judges knew the tactics of prosecutors and defense attorneys but somehow had an intuitive sense about how far they would let them go to discover the truth or to hide the truth through legal maneuvering.

Being a criminal attorney has always been, in my mind, a difficult job; it took a person with a flamboyant and think-on-your-feet personality, plenty of guts, and intimate knowledge of the law. On the other hand, prosecutors needed the ability to tie together all the loose ends that occur during the course of a criminal investigation and the ability to present facts and evidence in a clear and compelling manner.

During 1972, my first year of sketching for television, I met two prosecutors, John F. Kennan and Jack Litman, who later went on to greater fame in the legal community when they presented the criminal case against Bill Phillips, the so-called rogue cop of New York City. Unfortunately, they were overshadowed by the big gun brought in by Phillips: the renowned F. Lee Bailey.

That man was everything I imagined him to be. Although he was rather short with wavy dark hair sprinkled with gray, you thought that Bailey was seven feet tall when he looked at or spoke to you. He radiated self-confidence, and when his small, beady eyes focused on someone, those eyes glowed as if they were headlights.

Bailey blended his rugged handsomeness—a Clint Eastwood smile, a Kirk Douglas dimple, and John Wayne broad shoulders—with his knowledge of law into a potent force in the courtroom. He played off the fact that all eyes were riveted to him. Because he also knew he was a good attorney, he often tried to run the courtroom, and he commanded the attention of everyone with his boisterous oratorical skills.

Bailey mesmerized the place, but Kennan and Litman presented their case with skill and a bit less bravado, which resulted in a hung jury. That probably turned out to be unfortunate for Phillips, because I didn't think he could afford the services of F. Lee Bailey in another trial.

I met radical attorney William Kunstler in 1973 during the trial of black activist H. Rap Brown. Of all the lawyers I encountered in the courtroom, Kunstler was by far the most colorful and, in a strange way, the most flamboyant. He so enjoyed playing the role of radical and counterculture legal warrior in every manner, from physical appearance to courtroom antics.

I loved to sketch his head and face. He wore his graying hair long and stringy in front, and combed it back across a rather large bald spot on the top of his head. Kunstler also grew his facial hair into thick muttonchop sideburns, and his bushy brows accentuated hazel eyes that sparkled with passion.

This man certainly didn't know the definition of vanity. He dressed haphazardly and had terrible teeth. I frequently saw stains on his ties, his shirts looked grimy, and his suits were forever wrinkled. In fact, there was something quite comical about Kunstler; his melodramatic courtroom speeches coupled with his unkempt appearance made him, at times, the courtroom version of Groucho Marx.

At various times I noticed an undercurrent of resentment between Kunstler and black lawyers who represented other activists involved in the same case. I don't know if it was legal jealousy and competition or uncomfortableness on everyone's part because Kunstler was white.

However, there never was a question of Kunstler's dedication to radicals and to black activists. His commitment ran deep and never was a joking matter. He seemed to live by a statement he once made to *The New York Times:* "I only defend those whose goals I share," Kunstler said. "I am not a lawyer for hire. I only defend those I love."

Kunstler also had a substantial sense of humor, which sometimes was crude, and he never seemed afraid to use it. I'll absolutely never forget one incident that happened during the H. Rap Brown trial. I had asked Mike Pearl, a reporter for the *New York Post,* to keep an eye on my portfolio and sketchpads while I used the courthouse rest room. Because I had once found the door open and walked in on two men standing legs apart in front of the urinals, I knocked twice, heard no response, and entered the ladies' section—a single enclosed toilet.

Then I heard the bathroom door open and saw the shoes of a man as he approached the urinal. This sort of thing always had been such an embarrassment to me, but reason dictated that I quietly sit until the man finished and make my exit after his departure.

I froze when I heard William Kunstler's voice. "Ida," he said laughingly, "come on out and sketch it." I sat motionless and didn't say a word while he stood in front of the urinal, zipped up, and walked out. Then I got myself together for a fast exit. When I saw Kunstler again in the courtroom, I pretended the bathroom encounter had never happened.

* * *

ALTHOUGH I NEVER PERSONALLY LIKED THE MAN OR WHAT he stood for, I had a particular fascination with watching the controversial and now deceased attorney Roy Cohn work a courtroom. And he worked everyone in the courtroom. Cohn must have learned a great deal from his friendship and association with Senator Joseph McCarthy, who led the notorious political witch-hunt of the Cold War period. Cohn had served as chief counsel in 1953 and 1954 to McCarthy's Senate investigating committee.

When I observed Cohn in court two and three decades later, he was still so contemptuous of others. One time Cohn described Judge Irving Saypol as "the epitome of vanity, obsequious to his own superiors." Well, that was the perfect description of Roy Cohn himself.

To him, law was a game, and he considered the courtroom his personal playground. He knew many lawyers and judges so well that I believe he somehow used his knowledge of their personal lives, much of which he probably gained through overzealousness during the McCarthy years, in gaining favor for his clients.

Cohn, too, was an intriguing subject to sketch because of his physical appearance. With hair cut so short that he seemed almost bald and with huge blue eyes that almost popped out of his head, Cohn stalked about the courtroom with a menacing manner that gave the appearance that he was both angry and scornful. If he was your enemy, you had to watch your back. On the other hand, it seemed to me that if he was your friend, you had a friend for life. Perhaps that's why he had so many loyal clients in the world of entertainment and politics.

Although Cohn won many cases, he eventually "lost" two clients I sketched during criminal proceedings. He had represented Mob boss Carmine Galente on murder charges and obtained his release from jail. However, Galente was assassinated shortly thereafter during an organized-crime power struggle.

Cohn also had represented Adela Holtzer, who had been accused of defrauding investors through a Ponzi scheme that involved fictitious real estate and an auto dealership in Spain. As I understood the special circumstances of the case, Holtzer hadn't paid Cohn for his legal services, and he wasn't overly enthusiastic in his defense of her. In fact, this trial was the first time I saw a lawyer actually want to lose the case for a client. Poor Adela went off to jail, where she became friends with Jean Harris, and Cohn moved on to his next case.

But the most bizarre twist involving legal representation in a case happened during the Mob Commission trial, when reputed gangster Carmine ("The Snake") Persico decided to be his own attorney. The man, quietly advised by accredited lawyer Frank Lopez, gave a colorful opening statement and a closing argument to the jury in "fractured" English and genuinely believed that the government was not treating him fairly and that the charges against him were unfounded.

The scene was such a contrast to other mob trials, where highly paid and highly influential attorneys such as Roy Cohn, Barry Slotnick, James LaRossa, Harold Price Fahrenger, and Michael Rosen had organized a detailed defense for their clients. Persico actually didn't do too badly, even with his New York City "street" accent and phrases, but his power of persuasion failed to impress the jury because he was found guilty.

In many other cases, I noticed the calculated way in which attorneys sought to get sympathy and understanding for their clients. They frequently set up press conferences in the courthouse, where they made impassioned speeches about the innocence of their clients or about the special circumstances involved in the case. The defense lawyers tried to get sympathetic stories in the press to gain public support and take some of the heat off their clients.

Like it or not, public opinion and media coverage did have an impact on the way a case was tried or defended and, perhaps, even an impact on the verdict. One attorney was once quoted in the New York newspapers that if he hadn't gone to the press with his case, his client might have been lynched. I knew a number of lawyers who developed deep friendships with reporters for the sole reason of being able to get their clients' side of the story into the press.

Walter Bonner, who represented former secretary of commerce Maurice Stans in a Watergate-related trial, told me that he would even "streak" a courtroom if the publicity would help his client. That was the kind of importance placed on the right media coverage.

I personally found that newspeople played a great part in the condemnation or vindication of defendants involved in sensational trials. When the public screamed for revenge, it seemed to me that many reporters jumped on the bandwagon and condemned them in their stories. On the other hand, cases that didn't attract public attention usually moved through the system more expeditiously.

Despite its flaws, I discovered that the criminal justice system had a heart and that most of the time justice prevailed. The attorneys, be they defense lawyers, prosecutors, or public defenders, also earned my admiration for performing so well under adverse and dangerous conditions. Although truly horrible and morbid cases came across their desks, New York City assistant district attorneys were conscientious and brilliant.

However, I once became the object of an attorney's dangerous behavior while on assignment with a film crew. We were in a courthouse hallway when the attorney representing construction workers involved in the assault of other NBC employees actually gave me an uppercut to the jaw with his elbow. Although I was crying and this clown was two heads taller than I, I went after him, and the film crew photographed us. He claimed he didn't hit me intentionally and was trying to get away from seven television cameras. Well, that didn't hold much water with me because ours was the only crew on the scene. I wondered if anyone had ever told him that attorneys defend with words, not punches.

But what made me mad was the fact that NBC didn't press a case against the attorney. I was furious, but perhaps management thought one assault proceeding was enough.

Quick Sketches

Jacob Ezeroff, who represented New York City Patrolman Thomas Shea for allegedly killing a ten-year-old boy, hollered louder than any attorney I ever heard in court to make a point to the jury. No one slept during this trial because he raised the rafters, and the louder he became the more you believed his argument.

ONE OF THE MOST PATHETIC FIGURES I RAN ACROSS DURING my career was former Kings County District Attorney Eugene Gold. Although he hadn't tried a case in quite some time, he represented the county during the "Son of Sam" trial but pulled out of the case when several young girls accused him of sexual molestation, and the newspapers reported that he was a heavy drinker.

ATTORNEY RICHARD GOLUB, A HANDSOME MAN WITH BLOND hair and blue eyes and a natty dresser, presented a clean-cut and classy image for client Gary Gross, a photographer who had taken nude photos of actress Brooke Shields as a child. She sought to gain possession of the photos legally.

But I thought that Golub was more taken with himself and actress wife Marisa Berenson, whom he described to me as "the most beautiful woman in the world," than with the case itself. The court, however, must have liked Golub's legal act as much as his looks because his client retained possession of the nude pictures.

HARRY LIPSIG, WHO MUST HAVE BEEN IN HIS LATE EIGHTIES the last time I saw him in court, represented the lame and afflicted of our society. Known for his kindness as much as his skill as a negligence attorney, Lipsig assisted victims of crippling accidents in obtaining awards that allowed them to live with human dignity. Although he wasn't as flamboyant as F. Lee Bailey or as scholarly as Arthur Goldberg, I truly admired Lipsig for his compassion.

JUDGES, IN MY ESTIMATION, WERE A SPECIAL BREED. SOMEhow they maintained order while monitoring and pulling together all courtroom players and all the complexities of the law itself. Most judges also kept an open mind to the motions of both the prosecution and the defense. And even in the most serious and most sensational trials, they stayed cool on the bench and ensured the dignity of the proceedings.

But I was most impressed when judges gave instructions to the jury. They tried to put the law into understandable language, and they viewed the jury with respect. I often wondered how any jury could understand the ramifications of some statutes, but judges tied together all the loose ends into a neat package so that jurors could understand the law, yet have freedom of choice when it came to the verdict.

Most court clerks also held judges in a combination of

awe and esteem. The court clerks also served as an extra set of eyes and ears for judges. Since court clerks sat below and in front of the bench, they made sure everything ran smoothly, and they watched the courtroom for anything unusual that might affect the proceedings.

It didn't take me long to realize that judges are as human—and as vain—as anyone else. Once I became acquainted with them, judges usually arranged an excellent seat for me. I suspected that they did so because they wanted me to see the courtroom proceedings and still be able to sketch them well, too. One judge even asked me to go to the other side of the courtroom because that position provided me with his better profile. Other judges walked into court wearing business suits, turned to me, and said, "Ida, put a robe on me for your sketches."

Obviously, I tried very hard to keep on the good side of judges, because I knew that my freedom to sketch in the courtroom rested in their hands. And with the exception of the Canon 35 controversy in New Jersey, during which a judge confiscated and folded my sketches, I never gave a judge cause to have me reprimanded or dismissed from court.

As professional and respectful as most judges were, a few of them tried to bully me into giving them certain sketches they liked. They thought since NBC paid me for my time that I should give them my work for nothing, and they didn't realize that I, like any other artist, owned the pieces and only gave the network first reproduction rights. I usually sidetracked the demands when personally confronted by judges or their court clerks.

More often than not, though, I established an honest and warm friendship with judges. I respected and understood their role in the system, and they respected and understood my role as an artist working for a major media outlet. Frequently, they asked me into their chambers during recess, and I showed them my work, gave my opinion about certain aspects of the case, and talked. It gave them a break from the intensity of the trial; even judges needed someone to talk to in order to get through the day.

Being a judge was a tough job, and many of the men and women who served on the bench sometimes felt isolated, tired, and pained by the justice system. Judge Irving Lang, who presided at the trial of accused killer Jack Henry Abbott, provided a remarkable viewpoint of his work as a judge in a letter to me requesting several sketches.

"After difficult days in this department," Judge Lang wrote, "there are many nights I lie awake and often wonder what it is that keeps me in this position. I never find many answers, aside from the practical ones, of course.

"After talking briefly to you this morning, in the middle of a littered, dirty corridor with police barricades, I wondered about what a lifetime is—your children, your grandchildren, your eleven-dollar breakfast, and finally the fate of Jack Henry Abbott, who never will celebrate a happy birthday anywhere. For some reason on this dreary, snowy day in the midst of my business of crime, inmates, jails, and eventual deaths, you are a good reason I can survive all this stuff."

Quick Sketches

Judge Bruce Wright added to New York City's judicial legend because he released blacks and Hispanics, even if they were repeatedly arrested, without bail. He believed that bail was "a white man's measure of justice." That policy held firm when I covered the arraignment of a black man in Wright's court. When the judge asked for his name, the defendant claimed his name was Bill Smith.

As it turned out, Bill Smith was a bail-jumper who also used the aliases of Frank Smith, Eugene Smith, and Frank Johnson. Nonetheless, Judge Wright released the man without bail, and one of the arresting cops disparagingly said, "That's cut-'em-loose Bruce."

ON THE OTHER SIDE OF THE JUDICIAL SPECTRUM, JUDGE Sybil Harte Cooper ran a tough courtroom in Brooklyn, and if a guilty verdict was rendered, she gave the defendant a moral lecture about the crime and its impact on the victim and on society. I never saw her back down from anyone, including murderers and rapists.

THERE WAS, OF COURSE, ONE NOTED ECCENTRIC AMONG judges in the Big Apple. A district attorney had accused Judge Allan Freiss of taking home a woman charged in his own courtroom with killing and dismembering a man. The judge, a bachelor who said his girlfriend also had spent the night in his house, claimed he was unable to find proper quarters for the accused murderess, so he permitted her to stay overnight in his residence. He was swiftly dismissed from the bench.

TEN

The Media

I WILL NEVER FORGET THAT FIRST MORNING IN 1972 WHEN I passed through the lobby of the RCA Building and flashed my press identification card. I was quite taken with the fact that suddenly I was part of the largest NBC affiliate in the country and would be contributing my sketches to both the station and the network.

The whole thing made me somewhat dumbfounded as well as slightly star-struck. I stood next to Arlene Francis in the elevator, and since I knew some of her relatives in Philadelphia, I started what turned out to be a rather pleasant conversation with her. I was so pleased with myself for taking charge and talking with a woman who had been a television celebrity for years and felt equally good when the newsroom staff welcomed me to broadcast news. But I knew that I had "arrived" and was part of the NBC system because I had my own toilet key.

I soon became accustomed to seeing celebrities from all areas of news and entertainment, and it was fascinating to observe their informal manner. Once, two women very casually approached my desk in the newsroom. One was tall, dark-haired, and wore jeans and a halter top. I had seen halter tops on women at the beach but rarely as part of city attire, so I was quite surprised by the woman's appearance. She was very thin at the waist and seemed to have two perfectly shaped round balls for a bustline. The woman introduced herself as Racquel Welch and politely asked for directions to Dick Schaap's sports office.

Betty Furness, the former actress who was our consumer affairs reporter, also had an unassuming manner, and a certain elegance and grace radiated from her. However, it was amusing to see this popular and sometimes hard-crusted reporter knitting sweaters, which was a hobby, in a television newsroom during a lull in her schedule.

The affiliate and even the network operated in those days on a smaller and less grandiose basis than people think. Assignment editors in New York sat in simple glass-partitioned cubicles, and the news director, Bernard Schussman, had a small, unadorned room with tapes of all shapes and sizes, some of which weren't even labeled, piled everywhere.

His desk was cluttered with letters and notes while paper, pencils, and pens were strewn all over the place. I'm not quite sure how Bernard managed to get everyone into his office for story conferences, or how he found anything on his desk. But the smile on his face led me to believe that he enjoyed his work. What was more important, especially to an outsider like me, was that he complimented people who worked hard and produced solid stories.

The desks in the newsroom looked like tables, and old typewriters were positioned every which way on them, while most of the men worked in shirtsleeves rolled up. In some ways, they reminded me of the always rumpled Peter Falk in the NBC program *Columbo,* and senior staffers looked more like gofers than powerful news executives.

The hardest things to get used to in television news

were the salty language, which I often found so crude that it was offensive; and the cruel jokes and constant political backbiting among producers, directors, and reporters. I knew that sort of thing happened in every business organization, but the intensity of the politicking took me by surprise.

But no matter how intense that became at both WNBC and NBC News, the good people with talent stood out and advanced. At WNBC, Heather Bernard, a beautiful yet hard-driving woman who drank carrot juice throughout the day, always seemed to scoop other reporters. She had a special way with people and developed her contacts and sources, especially tough police detectives.

At the network, reporter Bob Hager, who perfectly understood what my job was all about because his father was an artist, moved so fast on a story that he earned the nickname "The Rabbit." He knew exactly what he wanted and how to get the information for his story. We worked together on many cases, and his professionalism showed when the stories aired.

Les Crystal was the president of NBC News for a good reason: He had a reputation as an executive with great news savvy and a man with a lot of honor and class. I always felt so gratified when I received a note of thanks or encouragement from him because he was the busiest and most stressed person at the network. He unquestionably knew how to get the best—and the most—out of his people, especially perfectionists like myself.

Producer Richard Hunt always knew exactly what he wanted and worked so hard to get it. For example, he laid all the groundwork and did a great deal of research for my re-creation of the Sacco-Vanzetti trial. All I had to do was follow orders and do my thing with a sketchpad. He got so much out of people, including me, because he cared about the quality of the news report.

As the years flew by, I witnessed a changing of the guard. More women appeared in the newsroom in all positions, especially as editors, and the tempo of everything increased. That was the big growth time in television news, and the competition for who got what stories as well as competition for audience ratings meant people in the business had less time to do stories or to exchange pleasantries.

Somehow, though, exceptionally talented people found their way into the power positions and made a lasting imprint on the station as well as the network.

The most creative team at WNBC consisted of Ron Kershaw, news director; Carol Clancy, producer; and Terry Baker, assistant producer. They threw themselves into their jobs. Ron, in particular, was involved in every phase of the newscast. With Associated Press, United Press International, and NBC wire reports, he frequently briefed me on a particular court case or news incident and then explained how he envisioned our total news package, including my sketches.

From my selfish perspective, the station utilized me and the visual format of illustrations for televised news as never before. During many events, NBC camera crews shot footage, I sketched away like a madwoman, and both products were used on the air. This approach brought the action of an event together with the specific scene that I re-created. One St. Patrick's Day, for example, I covered the parade and did sketches at St. Patrick's Cathedral on Fifth Avenue in New York City. Michael Flannery, an elderly man who was an Irish Republican Army supporter, led the parade. His appearance was quite comical because he draped a long, reddish lock of hair over the top of his head in a circle and truly looked like a leprechaun. Later, when he stood next to New York Senator Daniel Patrick Moynihan, you could tell there was no love lost between them because of their differing views on the Irish question. I zeroed in on those two scenes, and they became part of our coverage. The camera's lens and the artist's eye brought the best visual presentation to the air.

At other times, though, I became *the* presentation. Because of the importance and the secretive nature of the operation, our government didn't allow any coverage of the abortive hostage rescue attempt in Iran. With Ron Kershaw at my side with every piece of information we could get our hands on after the outcome of the mission was announced, I reconstructed the event on my sketchpad, and those scenes were used both by the affiliate and by the Associated Press that day.

I also reconstructed the descent of Skylab, our twenty-five-ton space research facility, as it dropped out of orbit and fell back down to earth; the disastrous fire in a Titan missile silo in Arkansas; and the twenty-fifth-birthday commemoration of comatose Karen Ann Quinlan.

When I provided the only visual material for a major national or international story, the assignment gave me such an adrenaline rush. Not only did I complete artistic renderings of a news event, but I also reached back into every lesson of my art training and every second of my instant portraiture experience to record a scene that could not be seen by me or by the world. There were few emotional highs of my entire life that equaled those "exclusive" sketches I did for NBC. After viewing those assignments on the air, I had a much better idea of what reporters and camera crews went through to get special access to newsmakers and why they smiled so and crowed about their accomplishments.

NO MATTER HOW MANY PROFESSIONAL BUSINESS ASSOCIATES you had in a company, especially the largest television affiliate in the country that constantly fed the network stories as well as personnel, you also had people at all levels with artificially inflated egos, bad manners, and nasty dispositions. I encountered all of the above from competing illustrators and from executives at my own station.

Although I had many positive and rewarding experiences with artists from around the country who watched me work in court and asked me about instantaneous drawing, there always were flies in the ointment. I contended with some artists who were envious and mean and who often tried to sabotage my work or make my life as miserable as possible.

For openers, they tried to prevent me from obtaining a good seat in court or stole my drawing pencils, pastels, and sometimes my eyeglasses. I even learned that these troublemakers looked over my shoulder in court and copied my sketches, while others pirated from previous trials sketches that had been photographed and used—with my permission—by newspapers and magazines, or that had been shown in art exhibitions. When I received artistic or journalistic awards (and there were many), some illustrators privately or publicly denigrated me.

Like anyone else, I could be a difficult person at times because I established high standards for myself, and NBC expected several sketches—not just one—of each trial I covered. But courtroom illustration was such an individual and personal craft that I didn't understand how a single illustrator working quietly but feverishly to complete a scene could possibly have any impact on the work or demeanor of others; once the judge brought the court to order, I was too consumed with sketching and with meeting a deadline even to notice my competitors.

ALTHOUGH I HAD BEEN THE "MOTHER CONFESSOR" TO A substantial number of producers and reporters throughout my career at NBC, I managed to stay out of the political battles that sometimes dominated the newsroom. I credited that achievement to the fact that I wasn't a career person who had climbed my way up the NBC ladder but rather an outside vendor on contract—an illustrator who wanted nothing more than to cover trials and to see my sketches on the air. I had no special connections to use in the politics of NBC, and I did my job.

That's probably why I didn't know that Ron Kershaw and Jessica Savitch, who died several years ago in a tragic car accident, were an "item" until I read *Almost Golden* by Gwenda Blair. As sad as it must seem, the book, which detailed her career and her death, carried a certain amount of old-fashioned television politicking. I'm sure some of those who worked with Jessica scored "markers" with their bosses for saying negative things and ganging up on a woman who wasn't around to defend herself.

That's how nasty the behind-the-scenes politics of television news can become. After Kershaw left the news department and moved into sports, he told me, "Oh, Ida, I just couldn't take anymore of t-h-o-s-e people. They're impossible."

At the affiliate and the network levels, there were two types of people: those who worked and those who manipulated. The workers, especially at the network, found so many ways to keep themselves busy; it seemed that the busier they became, the more energy they had. The field producers, in particular, often ended up writing scripts for newscast anchors or even for reporters.

On the other hand, the manipulators had the time to bad-mouth people. As in the courtroom when I wondered about the guilt or innocence of a defendant, I searched the eyes of anyone I thought to be a manipulator. Sure enough, I discovered that these people never looked at you when spreading their gossip about how rotten this or that person was, and their eyes darted all over the room to make certain the right people saw them and the wrong people didn't see their handiwork.

Their comments were frequently childish, but manipulators sometimes were downright vicious and dangerous. For example, a news director could often immobilize an important and well-liked reporter by getting subordinates to spread rumors and build a consensus against the targeted person for management to use in employment negotiations. These manipulators even told me whom to associate with and whom to avoid.

The situation became worse instead of better as television began to dominate news, particularly when live local feeds and satellite hookups brought instant coverage of sensational or important national and international events.

Every time a new station manager or news director took control at the affiliate, it also seemed that we were redecorating the newsroom and studio. I found the whole scenario very amusing; each change in design was so important that you would have thought Jackie Kennedy was redoing the White House. One day the assignment desk was enclosed in a glass cage; the next day it was on a platform. God only knows how much money they spent on remodeling certain parts of the newsroom and the anchor desks.

But one thing never changed: the offices of the field staff. Reporters worked out of tiny cubicles, and photos of them on assignment or their story subjects were plastered to the small walls surrounding them. I sat at a drawing table behind a thin partition as you entered the newsroom, but the table disappeared periodically. It always reappeared later with a broken base or a broken something.

As much as I hated to admit it, there did seem to be sexual and racial overtones at the affiliate level. Mary Alice Williams ran into trouble because of her skill as well as her beauty and eventually took refuge for a while at Cable News Network; an assignment editor, an obnoxious man with the foulest mouth I ever heard, once told a beautiful woman reporter who happened to be black to "get going, you black c—t" in front of everyone in the newsroom; and one producer or director always put extra lights on two black women to tone down their skin color while on the air.

Every once in a while, a new batch of "twinkies" arrived in the newsroom. They were young women who recently had been hired as office and administrative assistants and who spent a great deal of time in private office meetings with male executives. It wasn't difficult to figure out what was going on when you later saw the appearance of each person.

Once, when I expected to be part of a meeting with a news executive and walked into an office that had a gigantic peacock (the NBC logo) and a baseball cap with a crude insignia of this man's attitude toward business hanging from the ceiling, I found the man entirely unzipped. I stomped out to the man's secretary and said, "When he gets himself together, I'll go back in."

I guessed that everyone got what they wanted. Sooner or later, the "twinkies" settled into solid jobs with the assignment desk, Betty Furness's consumer team, or the various anchor support staffs. Then a new batch of women appeared in the newsroom, and the whole process started over again.

Despite the success I had in working with news executives and in capturing the images of the courtroom, the political infighting seeped its way down to the sketch artists, and I was confronted with some difficult decisions from 1985 to 1987, the last two years of my career at NBC.

In television news one never knew for sure what made a person a valued member of the organization one day and expendable the next. I was out of step with the abrasive people who ran the affiliate in those days. There also was no doubt that some of the carping from my fellow illustrators about Ida Libby Dengrove gave management the idea that it was time to retire me.

It was quite well-known around the station that I didn't appreciate bad language, and I thought the "unzipped executive" and his underlings intentionally irritated and provoked comments from me to show I didn't fit into their tone and style. If that was their intent, I'm delighted I bucked the system.

A station manager came up to me once and said, "I

understand that you don't like to hear the word f——k." I told him that he had heard correctly, especially when it was every other word out of someone's mouth. I also informed him that I was a lady, a mother of three grown children, and a grandmother, and I saw no purpose to that kind of obscenity in casual conversation or in the heat of meeting a deadline.

The single most painful moment of my television career came when I saw three of my sketches, one each from major trials—Baby "M"; Bernhard Goetz; and a New York corruption case, which I did for a business magazine—used on the air by WNBC with the credit line of another artist. The artist credited with my work was a good illustrator, and I had no understanding of why she and the station purloined my sketches. It boggled my mind.

I decided right then and there that I would never work for the local affiliate again. Since I was being sabotaged, I knew that sooner or later they would find a way to move me out in favor of another artist. What amazed me about the whole situation, though, was why someone didn't ask me to train another artist to take my place or didn't ask me to retire. I would gladly have done so, knowing that I was moving into my midsixties and understanding that a younger artist could better keep pace with everything.

The way the entire issue was handled was indicative of the personalities of station executives, many of whom are no longer working for the affiliate or in television news.

I later took some satisfaction in rejecting several offers to do courtroom illustration work again, and I returned three unsigned contracts to the affiliate. After getting out of the commuting grind and decompressing from deadline madness, I relished being home with Ed, my husband, who had coped with my crazy schedule in television news and had suffered through his own cooking for fifteen years. I also threw myself back into art, which included an adjunct professorship at Monmouth College, where I taught instant portraiture; and other cultural affairs on the Jersey Shore.

As for other television sketch artists, I wished them luck in a hectic business. I knew and worked with truly talented and great artists—Howard Brodie, Freda Reiter, Betty Wells—and always will remember their work and the trials we covered together.

Whenever I recall those years, I immediately think about my sister, Freda Reiter. Born as identical twins, we grew up in Philadelphia, and our red hair marked us as "carrot tops." Our lives followed parallel paths, and our parents fostered our shared interest in art. By the time we were thirteen years old we were making a living for ourselves in art and often had joint exhibitions.

Identical twins, however, are not total mirrors of each other. As is so common among siblings, we were highly competitive. Our differences were many. I was left-handed and Freda was right-handed. I studied at the Moore Institute of Art in Philadelphia; Freda, who had begun classes with me at Moore, entered the Pennsylvania Academy of Fine Arts. I later married a physician, and she married a dentist. I moved to the Jersey Shore, and Freda remained in the Philadelphia area.

She moved into courtroom illustration in 1970, two years before I began my career at NBC. Working as a sketch artist for ABC, Freda had covered the Black Panther trials in New Haven and New York and the My Lai trial and had sketched senators, government officials, and U.S. Supreme Court nominees.

I found myself in the same courtroom with Freda only four times during our television careers. We both were excellent artists. I thought I had the lighter touch and was better able to capture the emotional flavor of a person or a place. Freda, who died in 1986, was better able to capture an overall feeling of a subject with great graphic skill. I believed we were the best in the business, and both of us left our imprint on courtroom sketching.

I also knew I was much resented by my fellow artists because I seemed to get many of the awards and praise that involved courtroom illustration.

I never expected to earn two Emmys and four Emmy nominations or to be the subject of newspaper, magazine, and television stories. Like news events, it all happened so quickly, and I hope I handled the attention with dignity and humility. Several honors, like the one-woman show that the New York chapter of the Television Academy of Arts and Sciences sponsored for me, provided a great thrill and personal satisfaction. I certainly loved every second of that exhibition because the best reward for an artist is to be appreciated.

I'm very proud of the role I played for so long in the news business. In an age of fast food, fast living, and even faster television coverage, I served up a panorama of courtroom scenes of the most important and most celebrated cases of two decades.

And if my sketches brought some degree of meaning and humanness to the confusion and despair frequently associated with the legal system, I succeeded as an illustrator and as a journalist, because I wanted viewers to experience the emotion of the courtroom.

Epilogue

My work as a courtroom illustrator was the most exciting period of my life. It was much better than any book I've read or any movie or play I've ever seen. Truth in the courtroom is so often stranger than fiction. The bizarre, the impossible, the unforgettable, the unbelievable happened every day.

Many people have wondered over the years if my work was worth five hours of commuting per day to see and to record the proceedings of the most bizarre crimes of the 1970s and 1980s. The answer is a resounding *yes*. Since I've been a frustrated lawyer most of my life, working for NBC provided the perfect opportunity to blend art, my first love, with the action and drama of the courtroom, where I met the most influential people of the criminal justice system as well as the most celebrated defendants of recent history.

I've always thought that my sketches depicted the "human feeling" of a trial and that television viewers could experience the courtroom scene as if they had actually seen, heard, and felt the action. My artist's eye and hand focused on a person's face. To me, the face—particularly the eyes—gave away their secrets. Despite the evidence or the testimony, the eyes provided the real plot of the trial. I tried to portray honestly in my sketches what I sensed in a person's eyes. That set the stage for each sketch and made me aware of the other factors in a defendant's life.

More often than not, I found myself sympathizing with defendants because they were sick—mentally ill—or poorly programmed for life. People are not made in a day or a week. They are a lifetime of experience. I hope that one day most grown-up people won't act like children when they are in a court of law and blame others for the situations in which they find themselves. There must be something basically missing or wrong with our cultural and our parental structure because so many defendants have little idea of what's right and wrong or take responsibility for their actions.

Parents certainly can't be held legally responsible for the actions of their adult children, but parents should and must be held morally accountable for the values they do or don't instill in their children.

This issue transcends all segments and races of our society. The wealthy of our country often emotionally and morally neglect their children because they're "too busy" to give them the love and guidance they need growing up. The crimes of the privileged, such as the sexual assault and murder of a young woman in Central Park by Robert Chambers, is no less wrong and no less sick than the rapes and the murders committed by "Ivan the Terrible" Mendoza.

Despite the difference in the class and ethnic background of the defendants in those two cases, they seemed to have grown up like wild weeds without any sense of right or wrong and without a sense of respect of other people or themselves. This has become a grave problem within our urban areas.

Throughout the 1970s and 1980s, more and more teenagers drank to excess or got high on drugs and then seriously assaulted or killed another person. My fifteen years in the courtroom taught me that older nonstreet people—yuppies who coke out their brains during lunch breaks, after work, and on weekends—are no better. Sooner or later they'll end up commiting some crime to support their habit, or becoming a drain on society when they're broke and enter some publicly supported rehabilitation program.

In less than twenty years, the bizarre had become commonplace in our criminal court system. Fewer people of all ages, all classes, and all ethnic groups knew the difference between right and wrong and lived with a warped sense of reality.

What has happened to us, America?

I NEVER DREAMED AS A CHILD THAT ONE DAY I WOULD SEE AND SKETCH a murderer. Growing up in Philadelphia, the closest I got to one was watching a movie or a play about murder. For most of my life I didn't believe in capital punishment, because I thought that no man or no jury had a right to play God and take the life of another human being. I went to women's schools, where I was taught there was good and evil in this world. But I was not prepared to see and to hear the evil that presented itself daily in the courtroom.

No single trial had a greater impact on my moral beliefs, especially in the areas of insanity defense and capital punishment, as the "Son of Sam" trial. Although I didn't live in New York City, commuting into the city and being in a courtroom daily made me very much part of the scene.

That man snuffed out the lives of six young women motivelessly and set fires throughout the city. Why would a man do something so reprehensible? As I had learned from my firsthand courtroom experience, often it was "a voice" inside the defendant's head that told him to kill. Other murderers testified that God had instructed them to commit their vicious acts. With the "Son of Sam," a dog told him to kill.

The man's eyes indicated to me that he was in another world. Once in a while he'd come back down to earth and smile or acknowledge someone or something around him. Then he gazed again into a space that only he knew.

I found Craig Crimmins, the young man who murdered a violinist at the Metropolitan Opera, another stargazer. That, too, was the most distinguishing feature of Mark David Chapman, the man who killed Beatle John Lennon. His reason for shooting the music legend? Lennon kept him, Chapman, from being the "real" John Lennon. The "look" of John Hinckley, Jr., who shot President Reagan and terribly wounded James Brady, so closely resembled these other men that he seemed physically related to them, like a brother.

It was difficult for me to sketch and to listen to these lost souls and yet know that what they did was so unbelievably wrong and sadistic. More than once I wondered who or what had created these monsters. Despite the fact that I've been married to a psychiatrist for forty-eight years and knew that these killers suffered from mental illness, I also asked myself what society should do to protect itself from them.

What made matters worse, at least from my vantage point, was when a lawyer went all out to defend a client he knew was guilty—as in the Richard Herrin, Robert Chambers, and Gail Collins Pappalardi trials—and placed the blame for the crime on the victim by suggesting the defendant was "made" emotionally unbalanced by the victim's sexual advances or verbal teases before the gun "accidentally" went off.

With that defense, the case always got crazier. Yes, the defendant was insane at the time of the murder but is sane now or will be in the near future. Should the jury convict someone who lost control and killed someone? Or should the jury show compassion and confine the defendant for a period of time in a mental facility?

The insanity defense is so difficult to understand that everyone is uncomfortable with it. When all the psychiatrists finish testifying, the fact is that the defendant becomes secondary and the insanity defense becomes the focus of the trial.

Throughout centuries of Anglo-American law, the courts have held that you can't punish people who were mentally incapable of governing their actions and acted like a wild beast. But the standard test used in court to determine if a person is insane—the infamous McNaughten Rule (Did the defendant know right from wrong when the crime was committed?)—didn't work. Lawyers, judges, juries, and doctors were often unknowledgeable and confused about what constituted insanity.

Wouldn't it be more sensible to try the defendant and let the jury decide the case and measure out the punishment even in crimes of passion involving so-called respectable people who lost control momentarily?

I've always believed in compassionate treatment for those duly convicted of crimes under our justice system, but I also questioned who would protect society from beastly behavior of repeat offenders or serial killers. In my mind, once the die was cast—once someone, especially a multiple killer, murdered—there was no turning back. The killer probably would kill again and again if given the chance.

These people, whom I earlier described as social misfits, are such a burden on society. Considering all the testimony about his demons, did anyone ever think that David Berkowitz could be rehabilitated? Was there any doubt in anyone's mind that if released the "Son of Sam" would kill again?

And what about the hatred that erupted when doctors and law enforcement authorities had "control" over Berkowitz in the courtroom and still he screamed obscenities at the mother of one of his victims?

The insanity defense gave Berkowitz a strategy in court, but what defense did Mrs. Moskowitz have against the raving of a truly sick man? It seemed to me that perhaps the legal rights of society—and certainly the moral rights of Mrs. Moskowitz—had been turned upside down. The legal system had lost control of the defendant and itself by bending over backward to make sure a criminally insane man exercised all his legal rights. When the "Son of Sam" again took over the mind and soul of David Berkowitz, who ended up making unintelligible guttural groans and animal-like sounds in the courtroom, weren't some of his moral and legal rights altered because he had become something other than human in intellectual and emotional terms?

I'll never forget that sad and pathetic incident or the intense security given to the "Son of Sam." That security was paid for by the taxpayers of New York, who had no such protection as they endured the indignities of everyday life in the city. Where was the justice? People like Berkowitz not only posed a threat to society but also created a financial burden to it.

In my judgment, society should do away with these killers in a humane way, though I know many people will question the morality of executing a sick man.

Others no doubt will say that the death of a killer won't stop others from killing. That may well be true, but at the very least it would stop a specific defendant from ever going on another rampage. The act of murder speaks for itself, and it can't be excused any longer.

FINALLY, I WANT TO COMMENT ON THE ROLE OF COURTROOM ILLUSTRATORS in the media's changing coverage of trials. Public access to the courtroom through the use of still cameras had been banned in this country since the "circus" of the Charles Lindbergh kidnapping trial in the 1930s. But local and state courts recently have rescinded restrictions on the media and opened up proceedings to television cameras in an effort to promote the public's right to know what happens in the criminal justice system.

We now live in a genuinely high-technology society that consumes information and news with great vigor, and I believe that cameras in local and state courthouses are here to stay. However, I hope that courtroom illustrators always will be an integral part of the media's coverage of legal affairs.

I know from personal experience the strengths and weaknesses of both visual forms, and courtroom illustration brings a special dimension to television news that should never be overlooked.

Through my hands, eyes, and ears I put human feelings and perspectives into sketches that provided a good visual package for viewers, whereas a straight camera presentation was sometimes cold and lacked meaning.

The reporter decided with me what to sketch and always knew what was in my sketchbook and quickly picked the most important or most revelatory scenes for presentation. But when a camera was used exclusively, the reporter had to edit the tape and hope that the right scene could be found to illustrate the story.

By virtue of the different visual formats, the illustrator did things that the camera couldn't and vice versa. For example, the illustrator edited out objects that were in the way. For a number of reasons most courts also prevented cameras from shooting juries, while illustrators were free to draw them and their reactions to testimony unobtrusively.

Cameras and illustrators focused or zoomed in on a particular person or scene, but technology prohibited cameras from showing a close-up of a person as well as an overall scene at the same time; an illustrator placed a person in the context of the whole courtroom. Proper light also was critical for the on-air presentation of the camera; on the other hand, an illustrator created light through shading on the sketchpad.

People, even illustrators, also were less conspicuous in court than cameras. I think it is human nature to play up to cameras by focusing on the lens, smiling, waving, or otherwise looking good. That preoccupation was, in some cases, distracting to the proceedings.

But the camera worked very well recording the reaction of all trial participants going to and from court or during press conferences. As I've already stated, camera crews and the technology they employed made the illustrator look good. The ability to transmit live or taped images of my sketches to millions of television sets made my news career possible. That power was enormous and made a tremendous impact on how we all literally viewed court proceedings.

The camera and the illustrator complemented each other and provided television viewers with the best of both visual formats. Today viewers see an actual "picture" of a trial as recorded by the camera or see an illustration with the artist's "human" interpretation. In either case, the power of television has given us a better understanding of a particular case or perhaps even the legal system itself.